101 things to do BEFORE YOU GROW UP

Walter Foster Jr.

Quarto is the authority on a wide range of topics.
Quarto educates, entertains, and enriches the lives of our readers—
enthusiasts and lovers of hands-on living.
www.quartoknows.com

First published in Great Britain in 2014 by Weldon Owen.

Written by Laura Dower
Editors: Alexandra Koken, Gemma Barder, and Fay Evans
Design and Illustration: Dan Bramall and Katie Knutton

Published by Walter Foster Jr.,
an imprint of Quarto Publishing Group USA Inc.
All rights reserved. Walter Foster Jr. is trademarked.

6 Orchard Road, Suite 100
Lake Forest, CA 92630
quartoknows.com
Visit our blogs @quartoknows.com

Printed in Malaysia
3 5 7 9 10 8 6 4 2

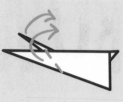

101 things to do BEFORE YOU GROW UP

CONTENTS

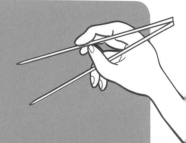

1 LAUNCH A PLASTIC-BAG PARACHUTE

It's a bird. It's a plane. It's ... a plastic bag!
Send your toys flying with this cool parachute.

YOU WILL NEED:

- Plastic bag or light material
- Scissors
- Needle and 4 pieces of thread—about 20 inches each
- Masking tape
- 4 paper clips
- Small object to act as the weight (a little action figure would be perfect)
- Rubber band

1 Cut out a large square from your plastic bag or material, and add tape to all four corners on the top and the bottom (8 pieces in total).

2 Thread the needle and push it through one corner, then tie the ends to a paper clip. Repeat for all corners.

3 Make a harness for your figure. Wrap a rubber band around it as shown, and then hook it onto your paper clips.

4 Find a safe high spot to launch your parachute, and watch your action figure float to the ground.

 DONE! DATE COMPLETED

MAKE A TIME CAPSULE

2

Making a time capsule is like building a cool treasure chest. Items are stored and sealed so that they can be rediscovered in the future!

most recent magazine or newspaper

clothes or accessories

DATE:
NAME:

a letter or diary entry

photographs

coins

toys

YOUR CAPSULE

You can make your capsule from any type of box. Mark your container clearly with today's date and your name, then fill it with cool items from your everyday life. Next, seal it and hide it somewhere safe. If you bury it outside, make sure you wrap it in plastic first to keep it watertight.

TIP
Never include perishable stuff (like food) that will get moldy or attract animals.

DONE!

DATE COMPLETED

3 LEARN TO JUGGLE THREE OBJECTS

Juggling is the perfect skill for showing off. With just a little focus, practice, and rhythm, you can be the star of any party!

SAFETY FIRST!

First things first: the main rule of juggling is safety, so don't even THINK about juggling flaming torches! Learn to juggle with small beanbags or balls. With the right objects and the right technique, you'll be ready to toss and twirl in no time at all—and you'll look pretty awesome doing it!

1 Grab a small ball or beanbag. Throw it from hand to hand in an arc. Toss it so that it's level with your eyes.

HANDY TO KNOW!

One of your hands is called the dominant hand because it does most of the throwing and catching. It's usually the hand you write with.

2 Throw the ball from one hand to the other without reaching out to grab the ball. Practice until you've got a good rhythm.

3 Now try tossing two balls at once. As the first ball is coming down, throw the second ball and catch both.

4 Now add a third ball, so that you're holding three balls in total. Your dominant hand should be holding two.

5 Throw the first two balls just like before, holding the third ball in your dominant hand.

6 Add a third throw just when the second ball is at its peak and keep throwing the balls in a continuous loop.

WHY NOT?
Substitute one of the balls for an apple. During the juggle, try to take a bite from the apple!

DONE!   DATE COMPLETED

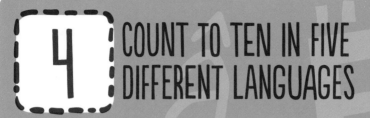

4 COUNT TO TEN IN FIVE DIFFERENT LANGUAGES

Thousands of languages are spoken across the globe. Impress your friends by counting to ten in five of them!

According to linguists (people who study languages) about 6,909 languages are spoken in the world. Wow! Study the numbers one through ten in the chart below (their pronunciation is shown in parentheses). Impress your family and teachers with your linguistic know-how!

	1	2	3	4	5	6	7	8	9	10
English	One	Two	Three	Four	Five	Six	Seven	Eight	Nine	Ten
French	Un (uh)	Deux (dyuh)	Trois (twah)	Quatre (katr)	Cinq (sank)	Six (sees)	Sept (set)	Huit (weet)	Neuf (nurf)	Dix (dees)
Mandarin Chinese	Yī (eee)	Èr (arr)	Sān (sahn)	Sì (ssuh)	Wǔ (woo)	Liù (liou)	Qī (chee)	Bā (bah)	Jiǔ (jeou)	Shí (shehr)
Spanish	Uno (oono)	Dos (dose)	Tres (trace)	Cuatro (kwah-tro)	Cinco (sink-oh)	Seis (sayss)	Siete (syet-teh)	Ocho (oh-cho)	Nueve (nweh-vay)	Diez (dee-as)
Russian	Odin (ah-din)	Dva (dvah)	Tri (tree)	Chetyre (che-terr-ee-eh)	Pyat' (pyah-ts)	Shyest' (shey-st)	Cyem (siem)	Voysy-em (vo-siem)	Dyevy-et (dee-eviet)	Dyeset (de-ee-siet)

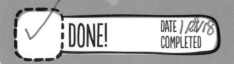

✓ DONE!   DATE COMPLETED / 20/18

TELL THE TIME WITHOUT A CLOCK

A sundial measures time by using sunlight to cast a "shadow-hand" over numbers. How cool is that?

YOU WILL NEED:
- Large plastic or paper drinking cup, with a plastic lid and straw
- Watch or clock
- Permanent marker
- Pencil
- Tape
- Some small pebbles (enough to fill the cup about halfway)
- Compass (See activity 12)

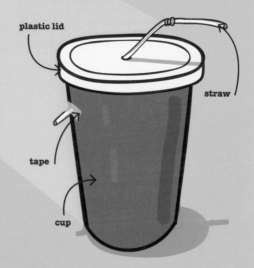

plastic lid

straw

tape

cup

1 Use the pencil to poke a hole in the side of the cup, approximately 2 inches from the top. Put the pebbles in the cup so that it doesn't tip over. Put the lid on the cup.

2 Put the straw through the hole in the lid and the hole in the side of the cup. Let it stick out about 1 inch from the side and tape the straw to the cup.

3 Find a sunny spot and place the cup on a level surface. Use a compass to find north and point the straw in that direction. Make sure that the sun shines right on the straw!

4 At 10:00 a.m., mark where the shadow from the straw falls on the lid of the cup. Repeat this every hour until 3:00 p.m. The next day you'll be able to tell the time without a clock!

DONE!   DATE COMPLETED

6 GET TIED UP IN KNOTS (OR AT LEAST TIE A FEW)

Here's the thing about knots—they are NOT uncommon. We use knots loads of times in our daily lives, so learning how to tie one is very important. Here are three useful and easy knots for you to try.

SQUARE KNOT

The square knot is used to tie two ropes together.

1 Lay the left end of one rope over the right end of the other. Pass the left end under the other rope and pull it to the top.

2 Point the ends inward. Pass the right-hand one over the left, then take it down behind it and up to the front, through the loop that has now been formed.

3 Pull the knot tight. To remember this knot, say, "Left over right and right over left."

BOWLINE (PRONOUNCED "BO-LIN")

The bowline is used to form a nonslip loop in the end of a rope. It was traditionally a waist knot used by climbers before harnesses were invented.

1 Form a loop in the rope by passing the working (bottom) part of the rope up and over the standing part (the attached part).

2 Pass the working end back up through the loop from behind, then around the back of the standing part.

3 Pass the working end back down the loop and pull tight.

CLOVE HITCH

Use this to tie a rope to a post.

 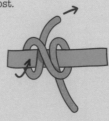 

1 Pass the working end over and under a post. Run it across the standing part.

2 Go around the post again, bringing the working end back. Tuck it under the cross.

3 Pull tight. The two ends of the rope should lie next to each other under the cross, in opposite directions.

DONE!

DATE COMPLETED

7 SEND A MESSAGE IN A BOTTLE

What if you wrote a note, stuck it in a bottle, and threw it into the ocean? How far would it go? Who would find it? See for yourself!

1 Find a medium-sized bottle with a strong lid to keep the water out.

2 Find some thick paper, if you can, and a permanent marker to write your note.

3 Write your message. Include an adult's email address so that whoever finds the bottle can contact you!

4 Make sure the tide is on its way out when you throw your bottle into the sea—otherwise it will just end up back on land. Off it goes!

DONE!   DATE COMPLETED

BUILD A SNOW FORTRESS

Build a wall of ice to hide your snowballs—then get ready for a real winter battle.

FOR THE WALL:

Scoop snow into a rectangular container (like an ice-cream carton), pack it down, then release it as a "snow brick." For a fantastic special effect, decorate your wall with snow that has been mixed with food coloring.

GUESS WHAT?

In January 2013, 5,800 people took part in a "snow-brawl" fight in Seattle, Washington.

FOR THE BALLS:

- Find perfect snow. Don't use snow that's too wet—you'll have slushballs instead of snowballs.

- When packing snowballs, be careful not to mix in twigs, rocks, or too much ice. You'll often find perfect snowball-snow closer to a curb or house where there's more heat—the snow will have melted a little.

- Frostbite alert! Wear warm gloves to pack and roll your snowballs. Don't barehand it.

- Aha! Your icy wall provides the perfect place to build up a stockpile. The ultimate snowball launch is firing two or three in a row. Splat! Your enemy won't know what hit 'em.

DONE!

DATE COMPLETED

9 MAKE THE ULTIMATE PIZZA

Eating a pizza is even better when it has all your favorite toppings—so why not make one yourself?

YOU WILL NEED:

- Oven
- Pizza-crust dough
- Pizza sauce
- Olive oil
- Cheese (mozzarella works best)
- The toppings you love! These can be anything from olives and onions to hamburger, sausage, or peppers.

SAFETY FIRST

Ask an adult to help you put your pizza in the oven and take it out again.

1 For the fastest pizza, go to the supermarket and buy some pizza-crust dough. Preheat the oven to the temperature listed on the packaging.

2 Put your dough flat on a pizza stone or baking sheet (drizzle the stone or sheet with a little olive oil first).

3 Spoon some pizza sauce (either bought or homemade) on top of the base. Sprinkle some cheese on top.

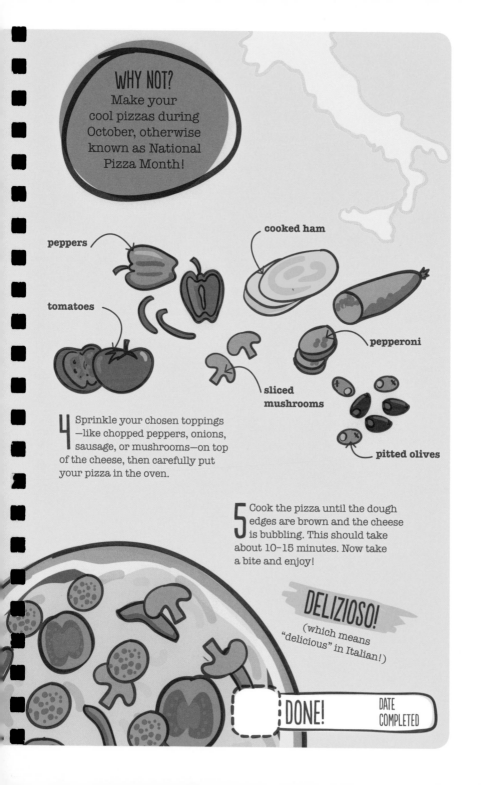

peppers

tomatoes

cooked ham

pepperoni

sliced mushrooms

pitted olives

4 Sprinkle your chosen toppings —like chopped peppers, onions, sausage, or mushrooms—on top of the cheese, then carefully put your pizza in the oven.

5 Cook the pizza until the dough edges are brown and the cheese is bubbling. This should take about 10–15 minutes. Now take a bite and enjoy!

DELIZIOSO!
(which means "delicious" in Italian!)

DONE!

DATE COMPLETED

10 INVENT YOUR OWN SECRET HANDSHAKE

Psssst! What's the coolest way for best friends to say hi? A super-secret handshake, complete with tugs, snaps, and other slick moves.

WHOOP-WHOOP!

1. 2. 3.

1 Decide on five or six moves for the handshake. Check out the list below and see what works for you and your friends.

2 Any secret handshake should involve all your senses. Add hoots, whistles, tongue-clicks, and a shriek or two.

3 Set an order for your handshake steps. Remember to add something unique to your handshake—a move you think of together.

WHY NOT TRY...

- Fist bump
- Clasp
- Pinky swear
- Touch fingertips
- Shoulder bump
- Fingers in the air
- Incy Wincy Spider fingertips
- High fives (up high and down low)
- High tens (that's with both hands)
- Hug it out
- Hip check
- Palm swipe
- Finger pulls

REMEMBER
Practice, practice, PRACTICE. You might have five or more steps in the handshake, but it needs to look effortless.

✓ DONE!

DATE No COMPLETED

DRAW A SELF-PORTRAIT

A self-portrait is when an artist draws him- or herself. Look at yourself in a mirror, grab a pen and some paper, and start your own!

1 To start your portrait, map out your features. Your hand is about as large as your face, so put your hand on the page.

2 Mark the top finger with a dot and then the heel of your palm with another dot. Connect them with an oval shape.

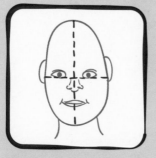

3 Draw a dotted cross inside the oval. Eyes sit on top of the horizontal line, the nose is at the center, and your mouth is below that.

4 Add more details, such as eyebrows, ears, and hair. Then erase the dotted cross, and *voilà!* You have a portrait!

DONE!   DATE COMPLETED

12 MAKE YOUR OWN COMPASS

A compass is a tool used for navigation. It contains a magnetized needle that responds to our planet's magnetism and points NORTH.

YOU WILL NEED:

- Straightened paper clip to use as a needle
- Bar magnet (a straight, rectangular magnet with a north and south pole on either side)
- Pliers
- Round piece of cork
- Small dish half-filled with water

1 Magnetize the paper clip needle by rubbing it against the magnet about 20 times in the same direction.

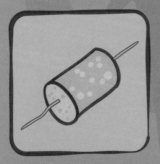

2 Using pliers, carefully push the "needle" through the cork. You need the same amount of needle showing on each side.

3 Place the cork and needle on the water. The end of the needle that points toward the sun at midday is pointing south if you are in the northern hemisphere, and north if you are in the southern hemisphere.

DONE!   DATE COMPLETED

WRITE A SPOOKY STORY

You know how to write an essay for school, and diary entries are easy, but what do you know about writing a frightening story? Here are four tips to make your next tale a real scream.

Start by scaring yourself silly. Face your fears head-on. What kind of story would make your toes curl? What do you see in your scariest dreams? Write about THAT.

What?

Choose a "what if" and go from there. What if you got locked out after dark? What if you faced a beast in the woods? What if your best friend was a vampire?

Where?

Choose a setting and add loads of scary details: fog, strange sounds, darkness, and more. Maybe make it so cold your characters can see their breath. Brrr!

Who?

Identify the main character. Who is he or she? Why are they doing in this scary setting? Create your villain. What does he or she look like? How does he or she act? Identify three moments of danger between the villain and your hero.

How?

Use the right words to scare your reader, such as "ghoulish," "terrifying," or "spooky." Take your time to present the details. Remember, half the work is creating tension! Tell the reader that bad things will happen, and then write them ... eventually.

✓ DONE!

DATE Nov, 11
COMPLETED

14 GO STARGAZING!

Constellations are groups of stars
in the night sky. There are at
least 88 different constellations,
each named after animals
or characters from mythology.

northern hemisphere

southern hemisphere

equator

WHERE ARE YOU?

The biggest constellation is called
Orion, also known as The Hunter.
How can you find it? Go outside in the
evening and look at the southwest sky
if you are in the northern hemisphere,
or the northwestern sky if you are in
the southern hemisphere. If you live on
or near the equator, Orion is visible in
the western sky.

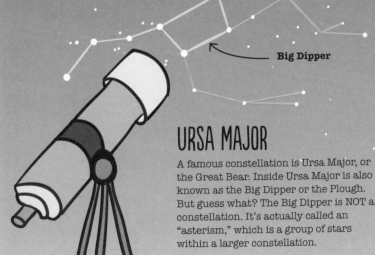

Big Dipper

URSA MAJOR

A famous constellation is Ursa Major, or
the Great Bear. Inside Ursa Major is also
known as the Big Dipper or the Plough.
But guess what? The Big Dipper is NOT a
constellation. It's actually called an
"asterism," which is a group of stars
within a larger constellation.

ORION

Look for the pattern of stars shown here (turn this page upside down if you are looking from the southern hemisphere). Three bright stars close together in a line are the easiest to find first. These three stars represent Orion's belt. Two bright stars above this are Orion's shoulders. The two below are his knees.

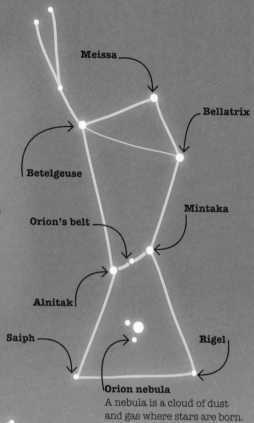

Meissa

Bellatrix

Betelgeuse

Mintaka

Orion's belt

Alnitak

Saiph

Rigel

Orion nebula
A nebula is a cloud of dust and gas where stars are born.

CANIS MINOR

CANIS MAJOR

Near Orion you may be able to see Canis Major and Canis Minor, Orion's two "hunting dog" companions.

WHY NOT?
Find out when you can see a meteor shower near you and spot a shooting star!

DONE!

DATE COMPLETED

15 BE A MYTH BUSTER

Put rumors to rest. Forget those superstitions. It's time to bust four popular myths!

Lightning NEVER strikes twice.

Although it seems unlikely, lightning *can* strike in the same spot more than once. The Empire State Building in New York City has more than 100 lightning strikes every year!

Touch a toad and you'll get WARTS.

Give that toad a break. Just because his skin is covered in bumps doesn't mean you'll catch warts if you touch him. His bumps are actually for camouflage!

Bulls get mad when they see the color RED.

Bullfighters wave a small, red cape to get a bull's attention. But believe it or not, it's not the color of the cape that matters to the bull—it's the movement of the fabric. In fact, bulls are color-blind, so they don't see the color red the same way as you or I do.

If you swallow chewing gum, it takes SEVEN YEARS to digest.

Food we chew and swallow is broken down by enzymes in the digestive system. But here's the problem with gum: its basic ingredient is designed *not* to break down when chewed. If swallowed, gum may take a little extra time to digest—but not seven years!

DONE!   DATE COMPLETED

MAKE SOME MAGIC

Presto! The easiest way to impress your friends and family is by having a few tricks up your sleeve. Try this one at your next party.

FLOATING KETCHUP

Before you start, empty a plastic bottle and fill it almost to the top with water.

1 Explain to your audience that you can make a pack of ketchup move at your command, then open the bottle and insert the pack. Close the lid.

2 With one hand, hold the bottle by the side so you can clearly see the ketchup pack. With the other hand, point at the pack, giving it commands as you do so: "Ketchup, up!" "Ketchup, down!"

3 The trick: As you tell the pack to move, gently squeeze the bottle. The water pressure will make the ketchup pack rise, fall, and even stop on command!

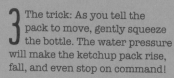

 DONE!

 DATE COMPLETED

17 MAKE SPOOKY BLACK FLOWERS

These flowers will look awesome displayed on Halloween, and they're super-simple to make.

YOU WILL NEED:

- White flowers (carnations or roses work well)
- Scissors
- Vase
- Black food coloring

1 Take your flowers and carefully snip off the ends of the stems.

2 Fill a vase about a third full of tap water, then add four to five drops of food coloring. You can use any color, but black is perfect for Halloween!

3 Put the flowers into the vase and leave them for a few hours, or overnight if you can. The flowers will soak up the black water and dye the petals black. Spooky!

WHY NOT?
Forgot to get some flowers for Mother's Day? Use this technique to dye celery sticks. Try pink food coloring instead of black!

MULTICOLORED FLOWERS

Once you've mastered this technique, try making two-colored flowers. Cut the stem into two halves with your scissors, then place each half in a different water-and-food coloring mixture. The petals on each side of the flower will soak up each color separately!

DONE! | DATE COMPLETED

18 BRING UP A BUTTERFLY

From egg to adult, butterflies undergo an amazing transformation known as metamorphosis. If you're lucky, you might just see this happen!

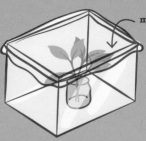

mesh material

1 Make a home for your caterpillar. Use a transparent box and cover it with mesh fabric (a fabric with tiny holes in it), so that there's something for the caterpillar to hang on to.

2 Find a caterpillar and invite it onto a stick. As you take it, pick a few leaves from the plant on which you found it. It will need these for food!

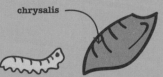

chrysalis

3 Place the caterpillar, leaves, and stick gently in your container, and put it outside in a sheltered area. In about six weeks you'll see a chrysalis, and soon, a butterfly.

REMEMBER
Once it has left the chrysalis, set your butterfly free!

DONE!   DATE COMPLETED

PLAY WITH SHADOW PUPPETS

You can make an entire zoo come to life on your wall, just using your hands, fingers, and some clever lighting.

SHOWTIME!

Shine a flashlight on an empty wall. The fun of making animal shadow puppets is practicing! Try different shapes and animals to see what looks best.

goat

alligator

rabbit

camel

bird

WHY NOT?
Put on a shadow puppet show for your friends and family!

DONE!

DATE COMPLETED

20 DRAW A COMIC STRIP

Comic strips can be funny, thoughtful, or packed with adventure! Here are some good ideas to help you draw your own.

1 Figure out what your style will be when you write and draw your comic. If you don't care so much about the details, that's okay! Draw stick figures and come up with funny punch lines or a silly drawing.

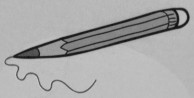

2 Draw your ideas in pencil first, so that you can make adjustments as you go.

3 Invent cool characters. Name them and give them simple and distinct features, like funky glasses, big hair, or scary teeth. What are their best and worst qualities? Funny comic strips need to end with a punch line, while adventure strips might end with a cliff-hanger!

4 Tell as much of the joke or story as you can through your pictures, and keep words in speech bubbles brief.

FACE FACTS

Show some emotion!
Here are a few secrets to drawing basic facial expressions.

Anger
A frown, slanted eyes, and possibly a red face.

Happiness
A smile and wide eyes.

Sadness
A frown and small eyes.

Shock
A gaping mouth, wide eyes, and possibly several lines near the forehead.

Mischief
A grin and slanted eyes, with one eyebrow raised.

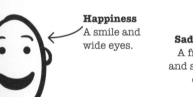

DONE!

DATE COMPLETED

21 MAKE TWO NATURAL INSTRUMENTS

The best music comes from the outdoors, like birds chirping or insects buzzing. Make these two instruments and get back to nature!

YOU WILL NEED:

- Cardboard tube
- Paint or colored markers
- Tape
- Paper
- Plastic or wooden toothpicks
- Scissors
- Dried beans

RAIN STICK

The rain stick is a musical instrument from South America that's usually made from the wooden skeleton of a cactus. Your rain stick will be a little different, but it should produce the same effect.

1 Take a cardboard tube (paper-towel or wrapping-paper tubes work well) and decorate the outside with paint, markers, etc. Tape a circle of paper over one end.

2 Poke some wooden or plastic toothpicks through the tube, following a downward spiral pattern. You should end up with something a lot like the image below. Secure the ends of the sticks with tape.

cardboard tube

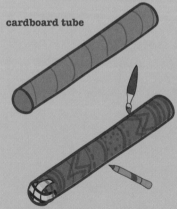

toothpicks

3 Drop a handful of dried beans inside, then tape another circle of paper over the open end. Tip your stick gently back and forth to hear the soft sound of rain.

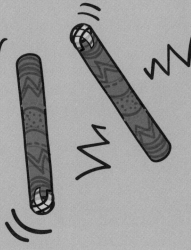

dried beans

GRASS TRUMPET

Make a funny, high-pitched squeal to, um, DELIGHT your friends with just a blade of grass and your hands!

1 Find a wide blade of grass. Hold up your left hand in a loose fist with your thumbnail pointing toward you. Then put your right hand next to your left hand with the blade of grass flat between your thumbs.

2 Hold the grass between your thumbs. Move the grass so that it is stretched tightly in the gap between your thumbs—and then move the gap against your lips.

3 Pucker your lips as if you were going to blow out a candle and blow hard into the gap. If you do it correctly you will hear the grass make a loud, squeaky sound.

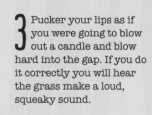

DONE!

DATE COMPLETED

22 INVENT YOUR OWN SUPERHERO

Flash! Zap! Pow! Use your very own superhero in a comic strip, or as the model for your next Halloween costume. Here are five things every superhero needs.

1 Motivation! There can be no superhero without conflict. What motivates your superhero to dress up and fight evil?

HELP!

2 An identity—or two! Give your hero a name that reflects his or her talents and strengths. Then come up with a daytime disguise!

3 A costume to fit the identity. A helmet, horns, or an oversized mask? A cape? A super-cool symbol?

✓ DONE!   DATE ??? COMPLETED

4 The villain! Heroes need someone to fight battles with—especially one who may launch a sneak attack to take over the world.

5 A tragic flaw and a trademark! The flaw is the one thing that can defeat a hero. The trademark could be something the hero says, like:

"PLANET RESCUED!"

WHY NOT?
Draw a comic strip about your new character. Check out activity 20 for ideas!

LEARN TO READ MUSIC

Reading music can be like reading a foreign language. Here are some basic tips to help you read notes and the speeds they're played.

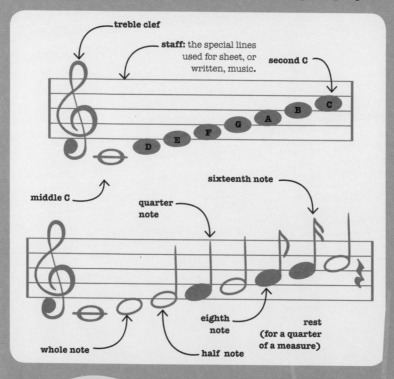

WHY NOT?
Learn to play a simple tune on an instrument like a recorder or piano.

 DONE!

DATE COMPLETED

24 MAKE SOME ROCK CANDY

There's nothing better than a science experiment you can eat! You'll definitely be sweet on this treat.

YOU WILL NEED:
- 2 cups water
- 4 cups sugar
- Pencil
- String
- Food coloring
- Lemon juice
- Glass jar

1 Tie a piece of string around the center of your pencil.

2 The string should be long enough to almost reach the bottom when the pencil is placed over the top of the jar.

3 Ask an adult to help you carefully bring the water to a boil, then add half a cup of the sugar.

4 When the mixture starts to bubble, add the rest of the sugar, half a cup at a time. Once the sugar has dissolved, take the pan off the heat.

5 Add a couple of drops of food coloring to your mixture and a squeeze of lemon for flavor, then pour into the jar, almost to the top. Place the pencil over the jar and let the string dangle into the liquid. Don't let it settle on the bottom or sides.

6 Find a safe place to leave your jar (not the refrigerator). After a day or so, you should start to see crystals forming around the string. Leave it for several days until more crystals form, then let it dry before enjoying your sweet treat!

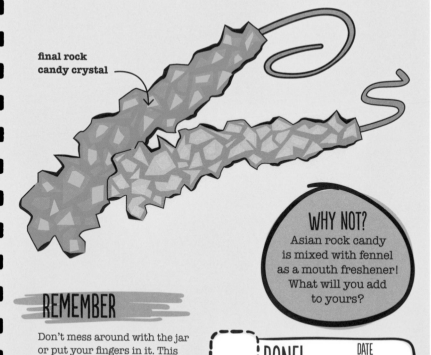

final rock candy crystal

WHY NOT?
Asian rock candy is mixed with fennel as a mouth freshener! What will you add to yours?

REMEMBER

Don't mess around with the jar or put your fingers in it. This disrupts the process of the crystalline formation!

DONE!
DATE COMPLETED

25 LEARN SOME DANCE MOVES

Bust some moves in front of a mirror, then show off your skills in the ultimate dance contest!

1 If there's one dance everyone tries, it's the limbo. A pole or broom is placed up high while the dancers shimmy underneath. Gradually the pole gets lower and lower. How low can *you* go?

2 Freestyle it! Dancers take turns showing off their best moves in the center of a circle. Try twisting, jumping up and down, and body-popping!

3 Learn a line dance. Get your friends in a line and see who can master the steps to an easy group dance like Gangnam Style. Or make up your own line dance!

DONE!   DATE COMPLETED

HARNESS THE POWER OF THE SUN!

26

Using a simple box on a hot day, you can focus the sun's energy and make an oven that will cook a gooey, tasty treat!

YOU WILL NEED:
- Shoe box
- Aluminum foil
- Plastic wrap
- Glue stick
- Graham crackers
- Marshmallows
- Chocolate

1 Prepare your shoe box. Carefully, cut a large hole in the lid. Using the glue stick, line the inside of the box with foil. Put the shiniest side facing up so that it reflects the sun's heat. Replace the lid.

2 Put your oven in the sun to preheat. After 30 minutes, put a graham cracker in the bottom with a marshmallow on top. Now cover the top of the box with plastic wrap.

3 Leave the oven in the sun until the marshmallow gets gooey and warm. Take it out and add a square of chocolate on top of the mushy marshmallow, then another graham cracker. Press down gently to mash the chocolate—and enjoy!

DONE! | DATE COMPLETED

27 MAKE AND FLY A QUICK KITE

There are many different types of kites, and here's a quick one you can make from a simple brown paper bag!

YOU WILL NEED:

- Brown paper bag
- Markers, crayons, or whatever else to design and decorate your kite
- Hole punch
- Four pieces of string 20 inches long
- Piece of string at least 8 feet long
- Tape
- Several torn pieces of crepe paper, each 8 inches long

1 Get the bag ready. Decorate it with markers and draw whatever you want!

hole punch

2 Open the paper bag and punch one hole at each of the four corners at the top of the bag. The hole should be about 1 inch away from the rim.

3 Push one 20-inch piece of string through each of the holes and tie a knot to keep it in place. Once you have attached all four strings, tie their ends together and connect them to your 8-foot-long piece.

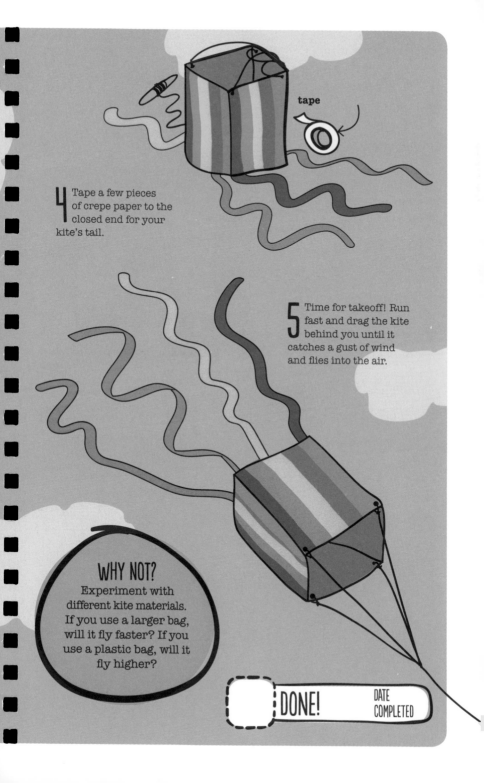

4 Tape a few pieces of crepe paper to the closed end for your kite's tail.

tape

5 Time for takeoff! Run fast and drag the kite behind you until it catches a gust of wind and flies into the air.

WHY NOT?
Experiment with different kite materials. If you use a larger bag, will it fly faster? If you use a plastic bag, will it fly higher?

DONE!

DATE COMPLETED

28 LIGHT UP A LAVA LAMP

Those cool blobs you see in a lava lamp are simple to re-create. And you can make them glow, too!

YOU WILL NEED:

- Clean plastic bottle with cap (1-liter bottle)
- Cooking oil
- Water
- Food coloring
- Indigestion tablet (broken into small pieces) or rock salt
- Flashlight

1 Fill ¼ of the bottle with water and the remaining ¾ with oil. Add about 10 drops of food coloring.

2 Drop in the indigestion tablet, and screw on the cap. Now watch colored bubbles rise as the tablet pieces fizz!

3 Turn out the lights and shine a flashlight under the bottom of the bottle. YOU made that cool special effect. Way to go!

DONE!   DATE COMPLETED

CREATE A SUPER PSEUDONYM

Sometimes famous authors write under a different name, called a "pseudonym." Making up a name can be loads of fun. Try it!

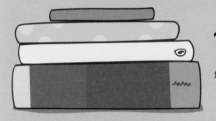

1 When selecting your pseudonym, you could mix up some names from your favorite books or movies.

2 Or you could choose a name that's an anagram of your own. Like this:

MIKE FOSTER
MKIEFSOTER
TOM FERSKIE

3 Why not add a fancy title, like Sir or Queen? Theodor Seuss Geisel adopted a pseudonym to make his mother happy. She wanted him to be a doctor, so he called himself Dr. Seuss!

WHY NOT?
Make up different names when writing a scary book, a joke book, or a dramatic book.

4 Try coming up with a fun, unique pseudonym signature. Practice signing your new name with swirls and zigzags!

√ DONE!

DATE 1/1/20
COMPLETED

30 REMEMBER ALMOST ANYTHING

Remembering things can be tricky, especially if you're studying for a really important test! Here are some great tips to help.

I BEFORE E, EXCEPT AFTER C!

1 Take your time and concentrate when you study new material. Create a picture in your mind. Make visual associations to remember names and words. Make up a song or a rhyme with the details you need to recall.

2 Create a story time line to remember an order of events or items. For example, if you need to remember sunglasses and flip-flops for a trip, you could say: "It was a bright and sunny morning when Mark bumped his toe."

3 Use a "mnemonic." This memory trick works like a nifty word puzzle. It's a sentence where the first letter of each word corresponds to another word. For example:

Never Eat Shredded Wheat reminds us of the directions on a compass in the order they appear, starting at the top: north, east, south, and west.

DONE! DATE COMPLETED

CREATE THREE COOL CODES

You've been chosen as a spy for a secret mission.
How do you plan to communicate?
In code, of course!

MAKE A CODE STICK

1 Take a pencil and wrap a long, thin piece of paper around it. Then write a message on the piece of paper. Once the message is written, remove the paper from the pencil. Your code will be tough to piece together to the untrained eye!

THIS IS WHAT
MIRROR WRITING
LOOKS LIKE.
NOW YOU TRY IT.

MESSAGE IN THE MIRROR

2 Take a sheet of paper and write a message while looking in a mirror. The letters should all be backwards. Without a mirror, the message looks like gobbledygook. With a mirror, the code message is instantly revealed.

CODE WORD: CHAPTERS

3 Many codes substitute letters for other ones. The one below uses the word CHAPTERS for the first eight letters of the alphabet, then lists the remaining letters of the alphabet backwards. Swap the letters in your code from Row A to Row B!

| C | H | A | P | T | E | R | S | Z | Y | X | W | V | U | Q | O | N | M | L | K | J | I | G | F | D | B | **Row A** |
| A | B | C | D | E | F | G | H | I | J | K | L | M | N | O | P | Q | R | S | T | U | V | W | X | Y | Z | **Row B** |

Can you figure out this message?
Z WQIT KQ MTCP!

DONE!

DATE
COMPLETED

32 FOLD AND FLY A PAPER PLANE

Ready for takeoff? Grab a piece of paper and construct your own awesome aircraft to send soaring into the sky.

1 Fold the paper in half lengthwise and open it up again.

2 Take the top right corner and fold it so that it meets the center crease. Do the same with the top left corner.

3 You should now have a triangle at the top of the paper.

4 Fold the triangle down toward the center of the paper.

WHY NOT?
Decorate your airplane with a unique design.

5 Take the right corner and fold it in toward the center. Do the same with the left corner. Make sure the two corner points touch.

6 Fold the paper in half along the crease you made in step 1.

7 To make the wings, fold the corners down toward the bottom of the airplane.

8 Grasp the plane from the bottom and launch it. Now watch it fly!

DONE!   DATE COMPLETED

33 DEAL WITH AN EMERGENCY

Handling an emergency well starts with being prepared. Know where to get help and how to stay calm when you need to.

FIRST-AID KIT

Have a basic first-aid kit packed and ready at all times. You can buy a complete kit, but check that it contains the essential items below.

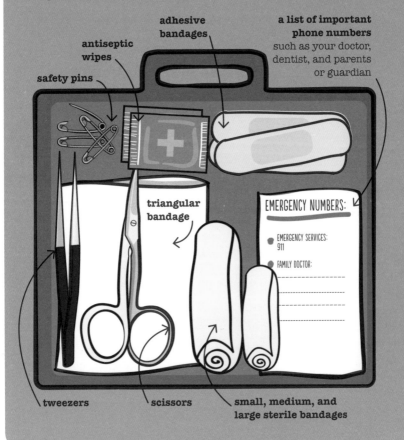

adhesive bandages

antiseptic wipes

safety pins

a list of important phone numbers such as your doctor, dentist, and parents or guardian

triangular bandage

EMERGENCY NUMBERS:

● EMERGENCY SERVICES: 911

● FAMILY DOCTOR:

tweezers

scissors

small, medium, and large sterile bandages

MAKE AN ARM SLING

Arm or wrist injuries can be very painful. Make your patient more comfortable by wrapping the injured arm in a supportive sling. If the injury is serious, make sure he or she sees a doctor or nurse, too.

1 Ask the person to sit down and support the injured arm, holding the wrist and hand slightly higher than the elbow.

2 Gently pull a triangular wrap between the arm and the chest so that one long end goes over the shoulder. Lift the lower part of the wrap over the arm and tie a knot beside the neck.

3 Bring the point of the sling by the elbow around the arm, and secure it to the back of the wrap with a safety pin.

SAFETY FIRST
If in doubt, call 911. The operator will tell you what to do.

DONE!   DATE COMPLETED

34 GROW A WORM FARM

Make your own worm farm and watch these squirmy creatures tunnel, eat, and make their way down into a new home!

YOU WILL NEED:

- Empty 2-liter plastic bottle
- Scissors
- Small pebbles
- Sand
- Soil
- Black construction paper
- Tape

1 Carefully cut the top off the bottle and tape the rim so that there are no sharp edges. Poke a couple of small holes in the bottom for drainage. (Keep the cut-off top—you will tape it back on top of the worm farm when you're finished!)

2 Layer your materials. Put the pebbles at the bottom, then add the sand, soil, more sand, and even more soil until you get to the top. Use soil from your backyard or a nearby park. Find some worms in your yard or buy compost worms at a garden center. Once the worm farm is ready, add the worms.

3 Wrap the black paper around the bottle to help re-create the worms' natural underground habitat, and stick the top back on with tape. After a day, check to see how far your worms have tunneled into their new home.

DONE!

DATE COMPLETED

BUILD A CITY OUT OF BOXES

35

Make an entire city using just the cardboard boxes you usually just throw away!

1 Collect a bunch of boxes of different sizes and widths. Best bets: cereal boxes, shoe boxes, smaller snack boxes, juice boxes, cardboard tubes, and spaghetti boxes (for skyscrapers, of course!). Wrap each box in paper.

2 Design and color your buildings using crayons, markers, and paint. Draw windows, doors, bricks, tiles, and whatever else you'd see on a building. How about plants, balconies, or a tiny photo of you inside one of the windows?

3 Place your buildings in an area together to make a town. Once all the buildings are in place, you can add even more details, like streets or a park. This city is limited only by your imagination!

WHY NOT?
Try making models of famous buildings, such as the Empire State Building, or the Eiffel Tower!

DONE! DATE COMPLETED

36 WEAVE YOUR WAY

Weaving has been around since the beginning of civilization. By making your own mini-loom, you can weave your own tiny tapestry.

YOU WILL NEED:

- Large square piece of sturdy cardboard
- Scissors
- Tape
- Ruler to measure and pencil to mark measurements
- Strong string or wool in different colors
- Needle with a wide eye

WHY NOT?

Use leftover wool to create a crazy colorful pattern!

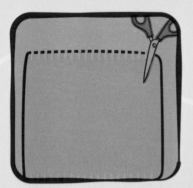

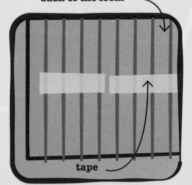

back of the loom

tape

1 Measure an even number of lines across the piece of cardboard about ½ inch apart. At the top and bottom of the cardboard, cut little notches for the string to sit in as you wrap it around the loom.

2 Choose a specific color for the string stretched on the loom itself. Carefully wrap the string around so that it catches in the notches on both ends. Then tape the pieces of string down on the back of your board, so that they stay put while you weave.

 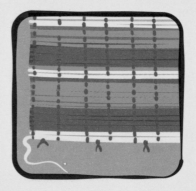

3 Choose another color of string. Using a needle, carefully begin to weave it under and over each string in turn. When you reach the end of a row, start a second row above the first, starting above the last string you ended on.

4 Keep weaving until the entire loom has been filled. You can change to different colors of string along the way. Carefully push each row together, keeping the rows straight. Remember not to pull the sides in too tight.

5 When you're finished, turn over the loom and cut across the taped-down string. Now take one end off of the loom and tie the pieces of string together in pairs to close the weaving. Your masterpiece is finished!

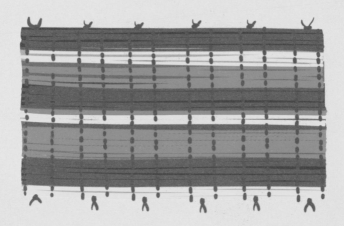

 DONE!   DATE COMPLETED

37 PREPARE FOR A NATURAL DISASTER

Hurricane! Earthquake! Flood! What would you do if you found yourself in the middle of a disaster? Here are a few survival tips.

SURVIVAL KIT

Be prepared before disaster strikes. Keep an emergency first-aid kit and a supply of nonperishable food (like cans of beans) and bottles of water so that you have them in case the power goes out. Don't forget to keep batteries, a flashlight, and a blanket in your first-aid kit, too.

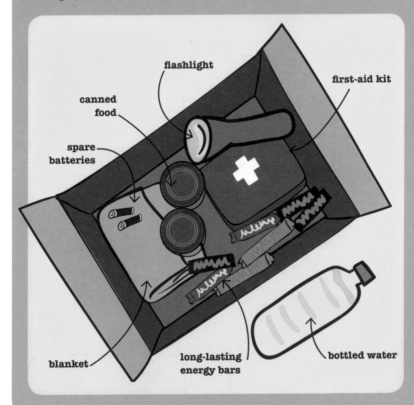

flashlight

canned food

first-aid kit

spare batteries

blanket

long-lasting energy bars

bottled water

GET READY

Many things can happen during a natural disaster that are beyond your control. The best thing you can do is know how to react when the time comes! Here are some tips for specific disasters.

HURRICANE

Fast winds may cause branches to break off the trees. Secure your windows and doors and move to a room inside your home as far away from windows as possible.

FLOOD

Heavy rains or storms can cause flooding in an area near water. Get as high up as possible in your home and listen to a local radio station for any evacuation orders.

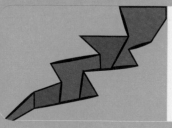

EARTHQUAKE

An earthquake can cause items inside in the home to move around. Stay low, cover your head with your hands, and crawl under a sturdy table.

TORNADO

Fast winds can devastate a small area. If indoors, stay on the lowest floor or move to the basement. If outdoors, lie down in a ditch.

DONE!   DATE COMPLETED

38 GET MAP SMART

Learn how to read three different types of maps.

TYPES OF MAPS

REGIONAL

Regional maps are the most common maps we use. They show us where places are and how to get from one place to another. You will find country borders or state lines, roads, and railways, as well as parks, lakes, and rivers.

POLITICAL

Political maps are color-coded to show different information such as population, languages, or countries. There is a key to the map, called a "legend," that explains what's being shown.

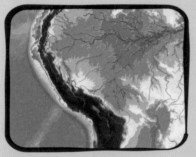

PHYSICAL

Physical maps show the way the land is shaped. Ragged, bumpy areas show where the land is mountainous or hilly. Green areas show where there are densely packed forests or jungles.

MAKE YOUR OWN MAP

Draw a map of your surrounding area using some pens, paper, and a few cool symbols! Include important things that can help you find your way, such as buildings, roads, bus stops, and green areas like parks. Once you've finished coloring your map, add the paths you use often, such as the one you take on your way to school, to a friend's house, or your local park.

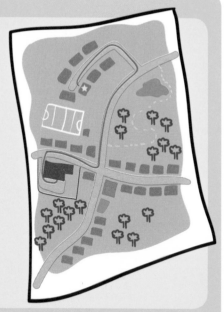

MAP SYMBOLS

Here are some important symbols you'll find in many regional or city maps. Can you add some to your map?

Train	Airport	Hospital or First Aid	Forest or woods
Church	Campground	Café or Restaurant	Mountain peak

DONE!   DATE COMPLETED

39 SPOT FIVE ANIMAL FOOTPRINTS

Locating and identifying animal tracks is really exciting. You just need to know what to look for—and where to find it.

1 Look for prints on soft ground. This could be mud, sand, or snow.

2 Tracks will be different depending on what the animal was doing. You can see whether it was walking or running, heavy or light, or even if it slipped!

3 Check out this chart to discover a few prints you may find in the wild, or even in your own backyard.

ANIMAL	TYPE OF PRINT
CAT	
DOG	
RABBIT	
SEAGULL	
SQUIRREL	

DONE! DATE COMPLETED

USE CHOPSTICKS [40]

Before eating, Japanese people say *Ita-daki-masu*, which means "I receive this food." Then they grab their chopsticks and eat! Now you try!

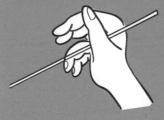

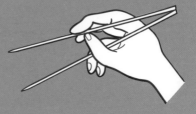

1 Hold your hand out as if you are about to shake hands. Place the first chopstick between the crook of your thumb and the top of your third finger.

2 Hold the second chopstick like a pencil with your thumb, index, and middle finger. Important: The bottom chopstick does not move.

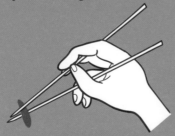

3 Use your thumb to hold the chopsticks firmly while you pivot the top chopstick to meet the bottom one. Use this motion to grasp the food!

GUESS WHAT?
In Japan it is considered rude to wave your chopsticks over your food. Go straight for the easiest piece!

DONE!   DATE COMPLETED

41 LEARN ABOUT YOUR ZODIAC SIGN

The study of astrology believes we are born under one of twelve different zodiac signs. Does your zodiac sign sound like you?

ARIES

The ram
(March 21st—April 19th)
Loyal, loves to be challenged,
and works hard.

TAURUS

The bull
(April 20th—May 20th)
Glamorous, dependable, but
easily embarrassed!

GEMINI

The twins
(May 21st—June 20th)
Talkative, charming, and caring.

CANCER

The crab
(June 21st—July 22nd)
Patient, protective, and a little shy.

LEO

The lion
(July 23rd—August 22nd)
Playful, ambitious, and loves being
the center of attention.

VIRGO

The maiden
(August 23rd—September 22nd)
Dedicated, organized, and
a perfectionist.

LIBRA

The scales
(September 23rd—October 22nd)
Great friend, artistic, but not good
at making decisions!

SCORPIO

The scorpion
(October 23rd—November 21st)
Intense, trusting, and great
at keeping secrets!

SAGITTARIUS

The archer
(November 22nd—December 21st)
Gentle, good attitude, but impatient!

CAPRICORN

The goat
(December 22nd—January 19th)
Realistic, generous, and thoughtful.

AQUARIUS

The water-bearer
(January 20th—February 18th)
Peaceful, inventive, and often quiet.

PISCES

The fish
(February 19th—March 20th)
Sympathetic, funny, and emotional.

WHY NOT?
Look up your
daily horoscope in
a newspaper or
magazine!

√ DONE!   DATE 1/29/18
COMPLETED

42 DO PUSH-UPS AND SIT-UPS

By doing these two simple exercises a few times each day, you'll give your body the tools it needs to stay strong.

PUSH-UP

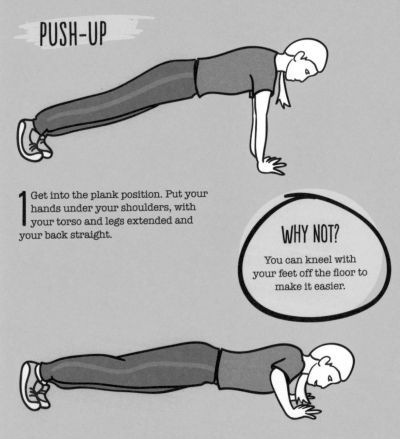

1 Get into the plank position. Put your hands under your shoulders, with your torso and legs extended and your back straight.

WHY NOT?

You can kneel with your feet off the floor to make it easier.

2 Bend your arms to lower your body. Don't stick your rear up or arch your back. You need to keep the strong "plank" position as you lower your body. Then push yourself back up again!

SIT-UP

1 Lie on the floor with your back straight and your arms crossed over your chest. Bend your knees, keeping your feet flat on the floor.

2 Using your stomach muscles, raise your back off the floor into a sitting position; then slowly lower back down to your first position. Repeat!

SAFETY FIRST!

Never strain yourself when you exercise, and stick to fewer than 10 repetitions a day.

Keep your feet on the floor!

 DONE!   DATE COMPLETED

43 UNDERSTAND YOUR DREAMS

Scientists still don't fully understand why we dream, but the dreams that we dream could have very specific meanings!

FALLING
You are feeling worried. Maybe it's about that big test that's coming up?

BEING CHASED
Someone is making you anxious.

INVISIBILITY
You need some love and attention.

FLYING
You are happy and feel free. Life is good!

TEETH
Lucky you! You might be rich one day.

MONSTERS
Something is making you feel afraid.

WHY NOT?
Keep a dream diary next to your bed. Record the details of your dream to analyze in the morning.

DONE!   DATE COMPLETED

PLAY THE INVINCIBLE BALLOON TRICK

Stick a pin into a balloon and it goes pop, right?
Amaze your friends with this simple trick!

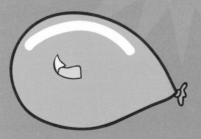

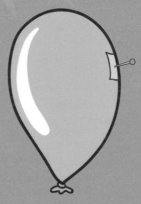

1 Before you show the trick to your audience, take your balloon and stick a small strip of clear tape to it.

2 Now for the trick! Hold the balloon so that the tape is facing away from your audience. Say the magic words while you take a pin and carefully (watch your fingers!) push it into the balloon through the tape. The balloon shouldn't pop!

3 Finally, to prove that the balloon wasn't a fake, stick the pin into the balloon and end your trick with a bang!

DONE!   DATE COMPLETED

45 BE A REAL "SEW-OFF"

Learn something useful and practical! Sew a button and a patch. Whoa, you are "sew" awesome!

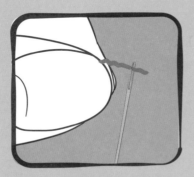

SEW ON A BUTTON

1 Cut 12 inches of thread the same color as the fabric you're sewing. Then push one end of the thread through the eye of your needle. Tie a knot in the other end to secure it in the fabric.

2 Place your button where you want it to go. Poke the needle through the back of your fabric and into one buttonhole, then stick it down through the hole that is diagonal to it. Repeat this step with the other holes. Do this at least six times, forming an "X" across the button holes.

3 Once the button feels firm, sew a few small stitches in the back of the fabric, behind your button, to secure it. Watch where you're sticking the needle —you don't want to stick it into your finger!

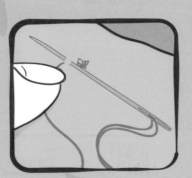

PATCH JEANS

1 First, cut a square of fabric that's 1½ inches bigger than the hole on each side.

2 Carefully fold the edges of your patch inward and pin the patch in place on top of the hole.

3 Sew small stitches around the edge of your patch to keep it secure. Be sure to watch your fingers!

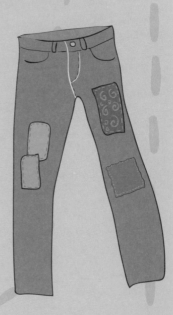

WHY NOT?
Choose crazy fabric to make your jeans stand out in a crowd!

DONE!   DATE COMPLETED

46 MAKE YOUR OWN THAUMATROPE

Check out this cool trick based on a 19th-century invention. It plays a trick on your eyes to create one awesome image!

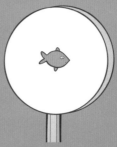

1 Put two cardboard circles on a table. Draw an empty fish tank on one and a fish in the middle of the other. Color both.

2 Tape the two cardboard circles back to back with a pencil in the middle. Leave enough room at the bottom to place your palms over the pencil.

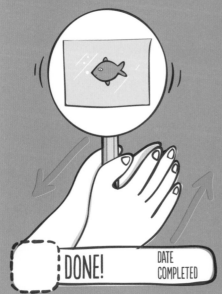

3 Place the pencil between your palms and spin it quickly. The images on the cards should begin to blend together so that you see the fish inside the fish tank!

HOW IT WORKS:

The illusion works best when the pictures are continuously visible. If you spin very fast, your brain thinks the images are one item. If you spin slowly, your eyes just switch from one image to another.

DONE!   DATE COMPLETED

BALANCE A SPOON ON YOUR NOSE

Try this trick at your next party! All you need is one spoon and a lot of concentration!

1 Grab a small spoon to perform your trick with.

2 Rub the concave side of the spoon on your nose to build up friction. Gently tilt your head back and keep rubbing. Once the spoon starts sticking to your nose, let go of the handle!

3 Having trouble? Breathe on it, or rub it a few times with your index finger before trying again. That should help!

WHY NOT?
Do something else while you balance the spoon. Sing a few verses of a song, dance around, or recite a poem.

DONE!   DATE COMPLETED

48 MAKE A FUNKY FLIPBOOK

Creating your own mini flipbook is like making a movie—but better, because you can make it with just paper, pencil, and your imagination.

1 Get a stack of thin paper that's easy to flip. A pad of sticky notes or a small blank notebook are perfect.

2 Choose your topic! You don't have to be a great artist—draw stick figures or a bouncing ball. Keep it simple!

3 Start at the last sheet of your pad and draw your first image. Go to the next page and trace it, changing it slightly as you go along to create the "movement."

4 Bigger changes from one drawing to the next will appear as faster motion when you flip. Smaller changes will seem slower.

5 Add a background, like rolling clouds and a sun, that changes position with each frame.

6 Once you're satisfied with your flipbook, outline the drawings in pen to make them easier to see. Now, start from the last page and flip through to watch your masterpiece come to life!

WHY NOT?
Add special effects! Put words flashing in the background, or a bird flying toward you!

DONE!

DATE COMPLETED

49 MAKE A SOCK PUPPET WITH ATTITUDE

You can make an effortlessly cool puppet from the simplest of items: a sock!

YOU WILL NEED:

- Large sock
- Piece of thick cardboard
- Scissors
- Wool (optional)
- Two buttons, googly eyes, pipe cleaners and whatever else you can find
- Fabric glue

1 Cut a large oval from the cardboard and fold it in half. This will be your puppet's mouth.

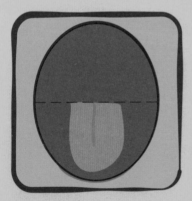

2 Decorate the oval so that it looks like a mouth. You can add a tongue, teeth ... even words!

3 Stick your hand inside the sock and find the "mouth." Put your thumb in the heel of the sock and your other fingers in the toes.

4 Dot some fabric glue inside the crease and insert the cardboard mouth. Leave to dry.

5 Finally, decorate your puppet with whatever other materials you want to make it more original: a fake wig (with wool), funny ears (with pipe cleaners), or perhaps a swatch of fabric for a cape!

wool hair

button eyes

felt tongue

WHY NOT?
Once you've made your sock puppet, give it a personality. Turn the page and learn how to make it talk for itself!

DONE! DATE COMPLETED

50 BE A VENTRILOQUIST

Now that you've created your puppet, it's time to make it talk!

BLAH BLAH BLAH BLAH BLAH

1 Capture your audience's attention by saying something as simple as, "Did you hear that?" The question will make them listen more closely.

2 Speak, moving your mouth as little as possible. You want to control your breathing and talk from "inside" your mouth.

3 Saying the letters B, F, M, P, Q, V, and W is very challenging. Try using the substitutions in this chart.

SOUND	TIP
For B	replace it with a "geh" sound at the back of the throat
For F	use a "th" sound so "fabulous" becomes "thabulous"
For M	use "nah" or "neh" instead so "master" becomes "nah-ster"
For P	use "kl" in the back of your throat, so "paint" becomes "klaint"
For Q	stretch out the sound so it's "koo"
For V	just like F, use the "th" sound
For W	use "oooh" at the start of a word so 'welcome' would sound like "oooh-elcome"

DONE!   DATE COMPLETED

SHAKE SOME ICE CREAM

51

You can make real ice cream with nothing more than a plastic bag and a few other simple items!

YOU WILL NEED:

- 1 small ziplock bag
- 1 large ziplock bag
- Lots of ice cubes (to fill a large plastic bag)
- 1 cup cream
- 2 ounces rock salt
- 2 tablespoons sugar
- ¼ teaspoon vanilla extract
- Yummy items to flavor the ice cream, like chocolate chips, nuts, or fruit

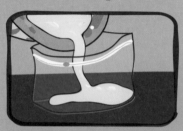

1 Combine the sugar, cream, and vanilla in a bowl and pour into the small bag. Seal tightly.

2 Put the salt and ice in the large bag, then put the sealed smaller bag inside the large bag.

3 Seal the larger bag. Shake until the mixture hardens. It should take about 5-10 minutes. Ta-da! You've got ice cream!

WHY NOT?

Add toppings to your ice cream once it's frozen. You could use fresh fruit or chocolate sauce!

cherry

chocolate sauce

√ DONE!

DATE ???
COMPLETED

52 HAVE FUN WITH PEN AND PAPER

Get ready for gaming fun! All you need is a pen, some paper, and a friend or two!

HANGMAN

Think of a word and give your friends the subject (such as a place, person, sport, movie, or TV show). For example, we've used "Italy" below. Next, draw a line for each letter in your word. Your friends then choose letters they think could be in the word, one at a time. If a letter is correct, write it on the appropriate line. However, if it's wrong, add a line to your hangman! Each friend tries to guess the word before the hangman drawing is complete. The steps to complete your drawing are pictured on the right.

SQUARES

First draw a grid of dots, (10x10). Now, take turns drawing lines between the dots. The aim is to complete a square during your turn. When you complete a square, write your initial inside, or color it.

CHARADES

You'll need at least three people to play this game. First cut or rip paper into little slips. Write names of books, TV shows, and movies on separate slips of paper. Now fold them and mix them up in a pile. Take turns pulling out a slip of paper, then "act" out silent clues to get your friends to guess what it is. There's only one rule—you can't make a sound! Here are ways to show what you're acting out:

BOOK

FILM

TV SHOW

YOU GOT IT!

DONE! DATE COMPLETED

53 INVENT A BOARD GAME

The next time there's a rainy day, don't just play any old game—design your own!

1 First design your board. The simplest board shape is square with 10 smaller squares on each side. Choose some of the squares to be "active" squares and color them.

2 Choose what kind of game you want. Do you like answering questions or doing dares? Come up with fun things to do each time you or your friends land on one of your active squares. Write them on small cards or pieces of paper and place them face down in the middle.

3 Before you start playing, make up some fun rules. Roll dice and take turns moving around the board.

TELL A JOKE!

DON'T FORGET!
You need game pieces to move around the board. Use beads, coins, action figures, or pieces of candy.

 DONE!

 DATE COMPLETED

DO A SKATEBOARD TRICK

54

One of the key tricks in skateboarding is a jump called the "ollie." Remember, **always** wear a helmet when ridng your skateboard!

SKATEBOARD PARTS:

nose
deck
kicktail
truck
wheel

1 Bend your knees. As you roll (slowly!), slam your right foot down as hard as you can on the kicktail and then jump into the air (above skateboard) with both feet.

2 As you go up into the air, drag your left foot up the deck. It will take time and practice to get the feel for this, so keep trying.

3 Bend your knees as you come down to soften the impact. Soon you will be doing an ollie like a pro!

✓ DONE!

DATE COMPLETED

55 LEARN THE SEVEN WONDERS OF THE WORLD

The most famous list of wonders includes seven ancient landmarks. Some remain, while others have disappeared over time.

1. THE GREAT PYRAMIDS OF GIZA

When? 26th century BC
What? Stone tombs built 755 feet wide and 480 feet high, with more than 2 million blocks of stone
Cool fact: Each stone block weighs more than a car!

2. THE HANGING GARDENS OF BABYLON

When? Unknown
What? Lush gardens with tree roots that grew into doorways and roads
Cool fact: There is no formal record of the garden, leading many to believe it was made up.

3. THE TEMPLE OF ARTEMIS AT EPHESUS

When? 6th century BC
What? Awesome towering temple built in honor of Artemis, the Greek goddess of hunting
Cool fact: The temple was destroyed by floods, earthquakes, and raids.

4. THE COLOSSUS OF RHODES

When? 3rd century BC

What? Enormous 100-foot-tall statue of Helios, the patron god of Rhodes

Cool fact: After a battle, leftover armor was melted down to make this statue.

5. THE LIGHTHOUSE OF ALEXANDRIA

When? 3rd century BC

What? The world's first lighthouse tower used to guide sailors at sea.

Cool fact: It used mirrors to reflect sunlight during the day. At night, men burned fires to create a guiding light.

6. THE STATUE OF ZEUS AT OLYMPIA

When? 5th century BC

What? Enormous throned figure of Zeus made from ivory, gold, wood, and other materials

Cool fact: The statue held a small sculpture of Nike, the goddess of victory, in his right hand.

7. THE MAUSOLEUM AT HALICARNASSUS, TURKEY

When? 4th century BC

What? Decorated with columns and sculpted carvings

Cool fact: Built for King Mausolus. The word "mausoleum," which means an above-ground tomb, comes from his name.

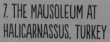
DONE!   DATE COMPLETED

56 BE A MAD SCIENTIST

By mixing ordinary items from the kitchen, you can change the color of liquids in a flash!

YOU WILL NEED:

- Mixing bowl (ideally glass)
- 7 clear plastic drinking cups
- Red cabbage
- Kitchen knife
- Approximately ½ cup of the following 7 liquids:
  - Lemon juice
  - Vinegar
  - Baking soda
  - Clear or colored dishwashing liquid
  - Ketchup
  - Lemonade or cola
  - Tap water

1 Carefully chop the cabbage and put small pieces into a bowl with 1 cup of water, then mash it with a fork until the water turns bright purple. Pour 1-2 tablespoons of the liquid into each of the plastic cups.

2 Add 1-2 tablespoons of the 7 liquids to the cups individually, making a note of which liquid has been added where. The liquids in the cups should change color!

THE RESULTS

When the cabbage juice turns red, it means that your other liquid (the lemon juice) is **acidic**. When the juice turns blue, it means the substance is **alkaline** (the baking soda). If the color doesn't change it means your mixer is **neutral**.

DONE!   DATE COMPLETED

Going camping requires lots of planning and organization. Get ready by reading this page!

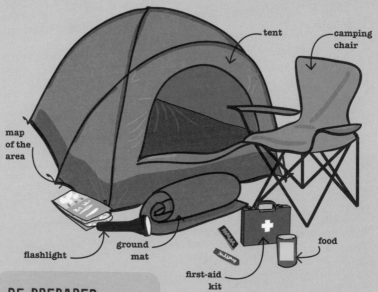

tent

camping chair

map of the area

flashlight

ground mat

first-aid kit

food

BE PREPARED

Pack essential items you need for a good night's sleep in the wild, such as a tent, a sleeping bag, and a ground mat. Think about where you are planning to camp and what the weather will be like, and take the right clothing to keep you warm. Also, remember a first-aid kit, food, a flashlight and a map for the ultimate outdoor experience!

SAFETY FIRST
Make sure that you tell someone where you are at all times, and never camp alone!

DONE!   DATE COMPLETED

58 BE A KNOW-IT-ALL

Impress your friends with your amazing knowledge. Here are some too-cool facts to share!

Like fingerprints, everyone's **tongue** print is different.

Only 20% of the Earth's deserts are covered in sand, while others are covered in **snow**.

Your **arm span** is the same length as your **height**. True story!

Frogs never close their eyes, even when they **sleep**.

It would take 1.2 million mosquitoes, all of them biting at once, to **completely drain** a human body of all its **blood**.

Most of the dust in your house is actually **dead skin cells**.

Cats sleep about **16 to 18 hours** each day.

WHY NOT?
Write down any new facts you find in your journal? Take a look at activity 60 to make your own!

DONE!

DATE COMPLETED

The clouds above your head aren't just there to look pretty. They can tell you LOADS about the weather!

CIRRUS

Cirrus clouds are the thin, wispy clouds often seen against a clear sky, formed by ice crystals. It should stay nice and dry for the time being!

ALTOCUMULUS

These clouds look like little clumps. A lot them together will create storm clouds.

CUMULUS

These are the big, fluffy clouds that disappear before the sun goes down. A lot of them can mean showers later on!

CUMULONIMBUS

When it's gray outside, it's probably because a cumulonimbus cloud is covering the sky! These clouds mean that it's raining where you are, or nearby.

DONE!

DATE COMPLETED

60 MAKE YOUR OWN JOURNAL

Writing in a journal is a lot of fun, and it could even help you become a great writer! Follow these simple tips to make your very own journal.

YOU WILL NEED:

- Heavy white construction paper
- Lined notebook paper
- Crayons, stickers, and markers for decoration
- Stapler
- Ribbon
- Hole punch

1 Take a piece of heavy construction paper and fold in half (like a birthday card)—this will be the cover for your journal, so decorate it however you like!

2 Now use a hole punch to make two holes halfway down your cover, close to the fold.

3 Take sheets of lined notebook paper and use your hole punch to make holes halfway down the paper on the left-hand side. These will make up the inside pages of your journal.

4 Place your notebook sheets inside your cover, and make sure all the holes line up.

5 Thread a length of ribbon through the holes in your cover and inside pages, then tie it in a bow.

6 Your journal is ready to use! You could also make one with plain paper to use as a sketchbook.

MY JOURNAL

WHY NOT?
Create a code that only you can understand to keep snooping eyes away from your journal!

DONE!

DATE COMPLETED

61 LEARN THE PHASES OF THE MOON

As the moon travels around the Earth it seems to change shape. These shapes are called phases. What phase is the moon in tonight?

First Quarter

Waxing Gibbous

Waxing Crescent

SHAPE SHIFTER

The moon looks like it's changing shape because the light from the sun hits it at different angles as it travels around the Earth. It takes 29.5 days for the moon to travel once around the Earth.

Full Moon

New Moon

Waning Gibbous

Last Quarter

Waning Crescent

DONE!

DATE COMPLETED

SAY "THANK YOU" IN 10 LANGUAGES

Be the perfect guest wherever you are by learning how to say "thank you!"

"GRACIAS"
Spanish

"MERCI"
French

"TAK"
Danish

"SPASIBO"
Russian

"GRAZIE"
Italian

"KIITOS"
Finnish

"EFHARISTO"
Greek

"DANK JE"
Dutch

"XIÈ XIÈ"
Chinese (Mandarin)
Pronounced
"syeh-syeh"

"ARIGATŌ"
Japanese

√ DONE!   DATE COMPLETED

63 MAKE A KITCHEN VOLCANO

Make your very own volcano with just a few items from your kitchen cabinet. Be sure to ask your parents first!

YOU WILL NEED:

- Modeling clay
- 1-liter plastic bottle with lid
- Red food coloring
- Dishwashing liquid
- White vinegar
- ¼ cup baking powder
- Warm water
- Plastic funnel
- Baking sheet

1 On the baking sheet, shape your clay around the plastic bottle to create a mountain shape. Leave the top of the bottle open and make sure nothing drops inside.

2 Mix a few drops of food coloring with water until it turns a fiery shade of red.

3 Pour the red water into your "mountain" opening using the funnel.

- The word "volcano" comes from Vulcan, the Roman god of fire.
- The largest known volcano in the universe is Olympus Mons, on the planet Mars. It measures 372 miles wide, which is as big as the entire country of Austria!
- One of Jupiter's moons is completely covered in volcanoes.

4 Carefully add six drops of the dishwashing liquid and all the baking powder into the mountain.

5 Now it's time for your volcano to erupt! Slowly pour your white vinegar through the funnel—you won't need much before the eruption begins!

WHY NOT?
Cover your baking sheet with sand and add some toy dinosaurs for a prehistoric volcano scene!

DONE!

DATE COMPLETED

64 TRICK YOUR BRAIN

These simple optical illusions seem straightforward, but some things are not always what they seem at first glance!

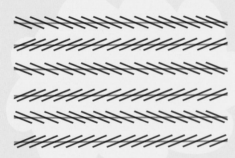

1 The red lines look like they're tilted, but are they?

Nope! They're perfectly straight! The illusion was discovered by German astrophysicist Johann Karl Friedric Zöllner.

2 Which one of the red circles below is the biggest?

Think you've got it? Well, actually they're both the same size—it's just that the small circles surrounding the one at the bottom make it look bigger.

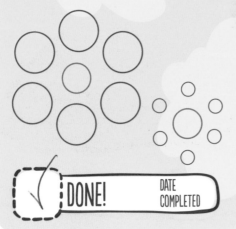

3 The grid above is made up of squares, but can you see spots?

This illusion is called a scintillating grid.

✓ DONE!   DATE COMPLETED

MAKE A SNOW GLOBE

Snow globes show a miniature scene with "snow" falling around it. Try making your own!

1 Take a small jar with a lid (a jam jar is perfect). Clean out the inside and remove all labels.

2 On the inside of the lid, glue down small objects like figurines or old board-game pieces. Use strong glue so that nothing will come loose inside the jar.

3 Fill the jar almost to the top with water and add a drop or two of glycerin (you can find this in the baking aisle at the supermarket). Now pour in a spoonful of glitter.

4 Carefully put the lid on the filled jar and screw it tightly shut. Flip it over and shake!

DONE! DATE COMPLETED

66 MAKE A SHORT MOVIE

Making a movie with friends can be a lot of fun!
Follow the tips below and create your
own masterpiece. Start with the four Ss.

SCRIPT

1 Once you've got an idea of your
story and characters, write a
script for each of your actors
to learn.

STORYBOARD

2 Make up a storyboard (a rough,
comic-strip style version of your
story) to use as a guide along
the way. Draw a quick sketch of how
you want each shot to look.

SPECIAL EFFECTS

3 Make-up, wigs, and other
costume elements can turn a
friend into a superstar actor!

SET AND SCENERY

4 You don't need to go to any
special locations to get great
shots. Your own house is an
excellent place to start. See if you
can get your family and friends to
be in your cast!

THE WIDE SHOT

Use this shot to show where the action is taking place and to set the scene.

OVER THE SHOULDER

This shot shows the action from your character's point of view.

CLOSE-UP

Use this shot to show your characters' emotions and reactions clearly.

EXTREME CLOSE-UP

This shot is great for focusing attention on small details. Using an extreme close-up of a character's face is a great way of creating a sense of tension.

 DONE!   DATE COMPLETED

67 BUNNY HOP ON A BMX

Impress your friends by mastering this awesome trick! Remember, **always** wear your helmet, in case you fall off.

1 Start by pushing forward slowly. Get ready to pull the front of the bike up.

2 Pull up the front wheel. As it starts to move back toward the ground, use your legs to kick the back of the bike up.

WHY NOT?
Get a friend to film
your new BMX skills.
For ideas on making
a short movie, see
activity 66!

3 With both of the wheels off the ground, you can hop over your obstacle!

4 For a smooth landing, bend your arms and knees as you land back on the ground. You should always try to land on the back wheel, or both wheels.

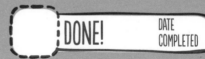

DONE! DATE COMPLETED

68 WRITE WITH INVISIBLE INK

Want to send a secret message to your friend? Here's one surefire way to get the word out— without anyone seeing a thing!

1 Dip your paintbrush or cotton swab lightly in the lemon juice and write a message on the white paper. Don't use too much; you want it to dry quickly.

2 As the paper dries, the message will disappear. Fold it up and give it to your friend.

3 To read the note, hold the paper close to a lamp. When the paper warms up, the lemon juice will magically reveal your message!

 DONE!   DATE COMPLETED

READ YOUR OWN PALM

69

For centuries, people have been telling the future by reading palms. Take a look at your own hand to see what's in store for *you*.

Girdle of Venus
Not everyone has one of these, but if you do, it means you are a sensitive soul!

Heart Line
Reveals your emotional side. If you have a wavy line, it means you are very caring.

Sun Line
If you have a strong sun line, it could mean that you'll be famous one day!

Head Line
Shows how you think about things. If it's long, you're probably very intelligent. If it's curved, you're creative!

Life Line
This shows your inner strength. The deeper it is, the tougher you are.

✓ DONE!

DATE ??
COMPLETED

70 CREATE YOUR OWN OBSTACLE COURSE

One of the best rainy-day activities is a homemade obstacle course! Use objects around your home to make yours.

START

1 Toy toss: Put a laundry basket at one end of the room, grab an armful of cuddly toys and pillows, and try to throw them in the basket. Get three out of five in the basket before moving on to the next stage!

2 Funny jumps: At this stop on the course, each player does a sequence of jumps in the air. Do a jumping jack, a frog jump, and a bunny hop.

3 Hula-paloola: Place a hula hoop on the floor and jump in and out of it ten times, keeping your feet together.

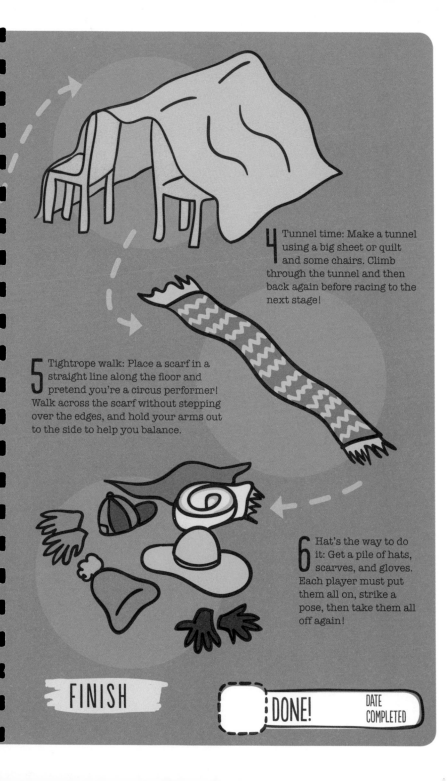

4 Tunnel time: Make a tunnel using a big sheet or quilt and some chairs. Climb through the tunnel and then back again before racing to the next stage!

5 Tightrope walk: Place a scarf in a straight line along the floor and pretend you're a circus performer! Walk across the scarf without stepping over the edges, and hold your arms out to the side to help you balance.

6 Hat's the way to do it: Get a pile of hats, scarves, and gloves. Each player must put them all on, strike a pose, then take them all off again!

FINISH

DONE! DATE COMPLETED

71 PAINT LIKE A FAMOUS ARTIST

You can create art in the style of some of the world's greatest artists! Here are two famous artists' techniques to inspire you.

SPLATTER PAINTING

The American artist Jackson Pollock used this technique to create some of his most famous works. Why not try it yourself?

YOU WILL NEED:

- Paper and cardboard
- Paints
- Paintbrushes
- Newspaper
- Tape
- Pencil
- Craft glue

1 First tape your newspaper onto the floor. This will keep the floor from getting too messy. Put your blank cardboard or paper on top of the newspapers.

2 Stand over the canvas and dip your paintbrush in the paint, then shake and splatter color from left to right. Do this several times with different colors.

IMPASTO PAINTING

Impasto is a way of painting where the paint is layered on so thickly that the brush marks can still be seen. The Dutch artist Vincent Van Gogh often used this technique.

1 Sketch the outline of your subject onto the cardboard using a pencil.

2 Paint with thick brushstrokes. Don't add water to your paint; you want it to be as thick and gooey as possible. Acrylic paint works best.

3 Allow the first layer of paint to dry before adding another. You can use the hard side of your brush handle to trace swirly patterns on the picture.

WHY NOT?
If you don't have acrylic paint, try adding a blob of craft glue to poster paint.

DONE!

DATE COMPLETED

72 MAKE YOUR OWN CHIA HEAD

These cool chia heads have hair you can eat!
Why not make a whole gang?

1 Take a clean yogurt container
and use felt-tips or paint to draw
a funny face.

2 Next, half-fill the container with
damp cotton balls.

3 Sprinkle some chia seeds
onto the cotton balls and
press them down gently.
Leave your chia head on a
sunny windowsill, but make
sure the cotton doesn't dry out.

4 When the chia has fully grown
you can snip it off to use in a
sandwich or salad. Yum!

DONE!   DATE COMPLETED

THROW A SUPER SLEEPOVER

Hosting a sleepover is so much fun!
Check out our tips for an awesome night.

THE INVITE

Make your invitation! These can be on paper, by email, or text message. Choose a party theme such as sports, music, or movie marathon.

FOOD

Stock up on your favorite snacks! Popcorn, chips, and vegetable sticks with dips are great.

STUFF TO DO

Make a list of games and activities that you and your friends like, so you aren't ever looking for something to do. Why not have each of your guests bring a favorite movie or game so that you have a big selection to choose from? You can also make up ghost stories after lights out!

SLEEP (NOT!)

Find the best place for everyone to get into their sleeping bags. Gather up loads of fluffy pillows and blankets and get comfortable!

WHY NOT?
Use some other activities in this book to keep you and your friends entertained!

 DONE!

DATE
COMPLETED

74 PLAY TRAVEL GAMES

Do you get bored on long trips? Next time you're on a long journey, why not have a go at these fun games? You'll be there before you know it!

EAT THE ALPHABET

Come up with funny things to eat for each letter of the alphabet. Announce, "I'm so hungry, I could eat an alligator." The next player continues with a B word. They might say, "I'm so hungry, I could eat an alligator and a beach ball!" Keep it going until you get to Z!

THE PLACE NAME GAME

The first person thinks of the name of a place (town, city, or country anywhere in the world)—for example, "London." Then, the next person has to try and think of a place name beginning with the last letter of that previous place name: for example, "Nepal." See how long you can keep it going!

NEW YORK

KENYA

GUESS THE THEME SONG

Each player takes turns to hum (no singing the words!) a TV theme song. The first person to guess the tune gets to go next.

 DONE! DATE COMPLETED

MAKE THE BEST HOT CHOCOLATE

If you've only ever tried powdered hot chocolate, you're in for a real treat!

1 Ask an adult to heat up some milk. Meanwhile, break up a small bar of dark chocolate into a heat-resistant glass pitcher.

2 Carefully, pour a third of the hot milk over the chocolate and whisk. Leave to stand for a minute.

3 Add in the rest of the milk, still whisking, until the milk and chocolate are completely combined. Enjoy in your favorite mug!

WHY NOT?
Sprinkle some mini marshmallows on top of your hot chocolate for an extra treat!

DONE! DATE COMPLETED

76 GO ON A SCAVENGER HUNT

Go searching for items and collect everything on your list before your friends do!

WHERE TO PLAY

Your backyard or local park would be perfect places to hold a scavenger hunt, but they work indoors, too. Once you've chosen a place to play, make sure all of your players know where they should be looking, and don't go outside that area. Always make sure that an adult knows where you are if your hunt is away from your home.

MAKE A LIST

Start by making a list of things for your players to find. Here are some suggestions:

ON AN OUTDOOR HUNT:

- Pine cone
- Flower
- Leaf larger than your hand
- Leaf smaller than your palm
- Something that smells nice
- Something round
- Feather
- Piece of bark
- "Y"-shaped twig

ON AN INDOOR HUNT:

- Toothbrush
- Book
- DVD
- Cushion
- Pillow
- Spoon
- Odd sock
- Rubber duck
- A clothespin

SECRET ITEMS!

Hide some funny items (like an old sock or a rubber duck) around the search area. Tell your players that whoever finds these bonus items gets a special prize! If you want to join in the hunt, ask an adult to do this for you.

THE WINNER IS...

The first person to collect all the items on the list is the winner! When everyone comes back, take a good look at your collection.

WHY NOT?
Give extra prizes for the biggest leaf, the most unusual item, and the nicest flower.

DONE!

DATE COMPLETED

77 MAKE YOUR OWN NEWSPAPER

Making your own newspaper is a fun way to sharpen your writing skills and get your imagination going!

THE FRONT PAGE

Each **front page** shows one or two **headlines**. Words in headlines are large and need to catch the reader's attention.

THE
WEEKLY WOOF

Date: Weather: Price:

DOG FINDS LOST BONE AFTER 2 YEARS
It was in the back garden all along!

Masthead

Name your newspaper and create a **masthead**. This will be the most noticeable part of your front page. Add all the details you would find in a real newspaper: date, weather forecast, and price.

Headline

Photo

INSIDE YOUR NEWSPAPER

When you have made your **front page**, you can make the rest of your paper. Fill out the pages with smaller headlines, more articles, and more stories. When it's finished, staple it all together—and it's ready for the newsstand!

Write your **article**. Your story can be about anything you like! It could be a made-up event, or something that's really happened to you or your family.

Article

MOM: "DOG WRECKED MY GARDEN!"

THE BEST BIRTHDAY CAKE IN THE WORLD!

Cartoon

Caption

WHY NOT?
Make a newspaper all about your family! You could send it to relatives you don't see very often.

Include photographs or drawings with **captions**. Think of funny captions to go with your images and make sure each image relates to your story.

DONE!

DATE COMPLETED

78 MAKE A TIE-DYE T-SHIRT

Be creative and turn a plain white T-shirt into a cool new top!

YOU WILL NEED:

- White T-shirt
- Disposable tablecloth or trash bags
- Fabric dyes in your favorite colors
- Rubber bands
- Small bowl
- Large bowl
- Rubber gloves
- Salt
- Plastic squeeze bottles
- Plastic bag

1 Cover your work surface with the tablecloth or trash bags. Roll the T-shirt up from the collar to the bottom and tie rubber bands around it.

2 Wearing rubber gloves, carefully mix the fabric dye with water in a jug (following the instructions on the package), and pour the mixture into your squeeze bottle. You can do this with as many colors as you like!

3 Put warm salty water into a bowl and dip the shirt into the water. Take it out after a minute or two.

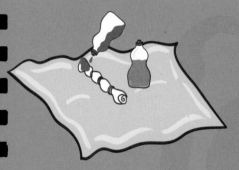

4 On your protected work surface, squeeze your fabric dye onto each section of the rubber-banded T-shirt.

5 When you have applied the color, put the dyed T-shirt into a plastic bag and leave it overnight. The next day, run your T-shirt under cold water while wearing rubber gloves to protect your hands. Rinse the shirt until the water runs clear, then remove the rubber bands!

6 Ask a grown-up to put the T-shirt into the washer (by itself!) and run it through a cold-water cycle. Then let it air-dry. For the next few washes, always wash this T-shirt separately.

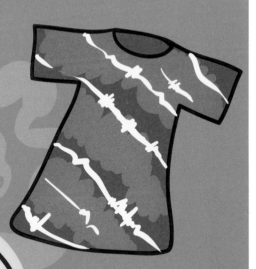

WHY NOT?
Try different colors and ways of tying your T-shirt to get different effects.

DONE!

DATE COMPLETED

79 MAKE A BALLOON SWAN

Turn a balloon into a beautiful swan and impress your party guests!

Twist here

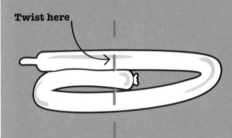

1 Inflate a long, thin balloon most of the way, leaving 2-3 inches at the end. Tie a knot at the open end. Bend the whole balloon into a large circle so that the knot is halfway inside the circle. Grab the balloon at the center and twist all the way around, holding the knot.

2 This will make two loops, and the part with the uninflated end should be poking up. This will be the swan's head. Fold the left-hand loop back through the right-hand loop to make a "body."

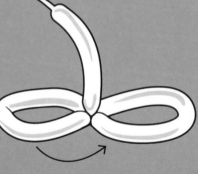

Squeeze here

3 While holding the top end, squeeze the air from the inflated part around the bend in the balloon. This makes the balloon stay in a bent position that's just right for the swan's head!

DONE! | DATE COMPLETED

Can you trick your own body? Why not test yourself with these amazing tricks.

APPLES AND ORANGES

Take an apple and an orange, and while taking a bite of the apple, hold the orange under your nose. How does the apple taste? Your sense of smell and taste are very closely linked, so you might find that the apple starts to taste like an orange!

THE TAP TEST

Place your hand palm down on a flat surface, like a tabletop. Without moving your other fingers try tapping your third finger. Easy, right? Now tuck your middle finger under your palm and try again. You should find it impossible to move! This is because your second and third fingers share a tendon.

WHY NOT?
Put on a magic show for your family and friends. See page 16 for more ideas.

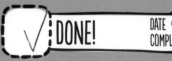

DONE!

DATE COMPLETED

81 MAKE A GUM-WRAPPER BRACELET

This bracelet is not only fun to make—you're also recycling! You can make this bracelet from any candy wrapper or scrap paper, but chewing gum wrappers are perfect.

1 Fold one long side in toward the middle of the wrapper, then do the same with the other side. Next fold the whole thing in half lengthwise to form a thin strip.

2 Bend your wrapper in the middle, then fold each long end in to meet in the middle.

3 Repeat steps 1-2 with your next piece of wrapper. Using different colors will create a pattern.

4 Insert the flat ends of one folded wrapper into the side openings of the next, so that they slot into each other and make a "V" shape.

5 Repeat the first four steps with your folded wrappers to form a zigzag chain.

6 When your bracelet is long enough to fit around your wrist, make one more link, but don't make the last two folds.

7 Insert these sides into the openings of your first wrapper, and close the bracelet by folding in the long strips. After a bit of practice your bracelet should look like this!

WHY NOT?
Try different color combinations and make bracelets for all of your friends!

DONE!

DATE COMPLETED

82 WALK THROUGH PAPER

Amaze your friends by walking through a single sheet of paper!

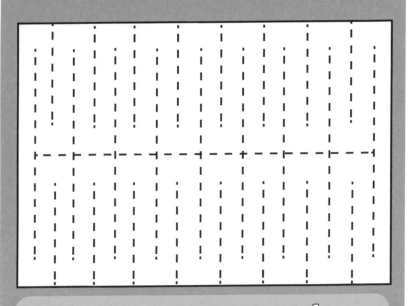

THE PERFORMANCE

1 Ask the audience if they think you can walk through a hole cut in an 8½ x 11-inch piece of paper.

2 Cut along the lines carefully in front of the audience. Tell some jokes to keep them entertained!

3 Stretch the paper apart carefully and walk through it. Ta-da!

DONE! DATE COMPLETED

MAKE PAPER-CUP SPEAKERS

Make your own handy pair of paper-cup speakers for your phone or MP3 player!

YOU WILL NEED:

- A pair of ear-bud heaphones
- Four paper drinking cups
- Two toothpicks
- Clear tape
- Small pair of scissors

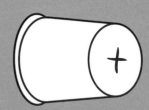

1 Using the toothpicks, carefully make a small, cross-shaped slit in the base of the two cups that will be the speakers.

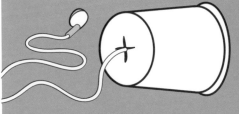

2 Insert the ear buds all the way through the holes, until only the wire is left outside the cup.

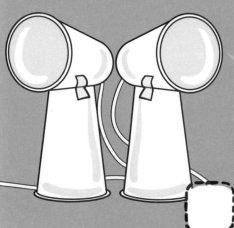

3 Turn the remaining cups upside down, then place your "speakers" sideways on top. Tape the sides to secure them in place. Plug the ear buds into an MP3 player and play some tunes!

DONE!

DATE COMPLETED

84 BLOW GIANT BUBBLES

Make your own oversized wand to blow gigantic bubbles!

YOU WILL NEED:

For the bubble solution:

- 3 cups water
- ¼ cup dishwashing liquid
- ½ cup cornstarch
- 1 tablespoon baking powder
- 1 tablespoon light corn syrup

For your super-bubble wand:

- 2 plastic straws
- String
- Tape measure
- Scissors
- Large plastic bowl

1 Measure 6½ feet of string, and thread it through both straws. Tie the ends of your string together, then space out your straws to make the handles of your bubble wand.

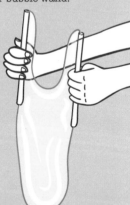

2 Put all of the ingredients for your bubble mixture into a large bowl and mix them well.

3 Dip your bubble wand into the mixture. Raise it into the air, and slowly walk backwards. Don't worry if it doesn't work the first time—you'll soon be making mind-blowing bubbles!

DONE!   DATE COMPLETED

MAKE GLOW-IN-THE-DARK GOO

Make a batch of crazy, glow-in-the-dark gloop!

YOU WILL NEED:

- 1¼ cups water
- Glow-in-the-dark paint
  (you can get this from art and
  craft stores)
- 2¼ cups cornstarch
- Bowl
- Wooden spoon
- Measuring cups

1 Mix the cornstarch with water, a little at a time. Stir until the mixture becomes dough-like.

2 Add the glow-in-the-dark paint. Mix again until it's completely mixed together.

3 Once your slime is ready to handle, hold it close to a light to activate the glow-in-the-dark magic.

TIP
Don't forget to wash your hands when you are finished, and store any leftover slime in a sealed sandwich bag.

DONE!

DATE COMPLETED

86 GO ON A GHOST HUNT

Want a scary adventure? Grab some friends and search for ghosts! Here's how to track down spirits lurking in your neighborhood...

GET READY

Once you're in the room or space that you're ghost-hunting in, be as calm and peaceful as possible. Turn out the lights, or dim them if you're feeling a bit nervous! Take notes of everything you see, hear, and feel.

ASK QUESTIONS

Once the room or space is as quiet as possible, ask the ghosts questions, such as, "Is anyone there?" or "Can you give us a sign?" See what happens after you've asked your question.

"IS ANYBODY THERE?"

UH-OH!

Once you've heard, felt, or spotted a ghost, ask around to see if anyone else has had the same experience. If you start getting too spooked, just say, "Spirit, I release you!" and turn on the lights. Compare notes with your friends to see if you have experienced a ghostly encounter!

SERIOUS SPOOKS!

Edinburgh, Scotland
The famous Edinburgh Playhouse has a friendly ghost called Albert, who wears a gray coat. He's believed to be an old stagehand who can't resist helping out now and then!

Bhanghar Fort, India
People say a wizard put a curse on this Indian village, and soon after that, the place was invaded. To this day, people think that the ghosts keep nosy visitors away.

Charles Bridge, Prague
In the Middle Ages, ten lords and noblemen were beheaded on this bridge. Their ghosts still linger there, singing in the night to scare off anyone who dares to cross the bridge.

SAFETY FIRST!

Remember, always tell an adult where you're going and never go out alone at night.

WHY NOT?
Bring along a camera and see if you can record any spooky occurrences!

DONE!

DATE COMPLETED

87 PRINT A BLOCK PICTURE

The next time your meal comes in a box, hold on to it.
You can use it to make a cool piece of art!

YOU WILL NEED:

- Leftover food container
- Pencil
- Plate
- Poster paint
- Paper
- Paint roller

1 Lightly sketch your design on one of the flat sides of your food box. When you are happy with it, press harder with your pencil to leave an imprint.

2 Put your paint on your plate and dip your roller into it. Make sure all the of roller wheel is lightly and evenly covered in paint.

3 Roll the paint onto the box, making sure you have covered the whole surface. Try not to put the paint on too thickly, or your design won't show.

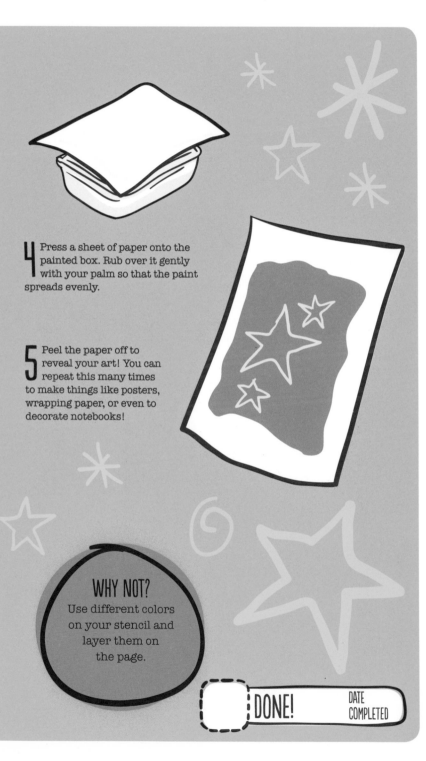

4 Press a sheet of paper onto the painted box. Rub over it gently with your palm so that the paint spreads evenly.

5 Peel the paper off to reveal your art! You can repeat this many times to make things like posters, wrapping paper, or even to decorate notebooks!

WHY NOT?
Use different colors on your stencil and layer them on the page.

DONE!

DATE COMPLETED

88 BE A HUMAN LIE DETECTOR

Follow these tips to uncover untruths!

BODY LANGUAGE CHECKLIST:

Read their body language! Check out these classic liar's traits.

✓ **Touching the face**
✓ **Rubbing the back of neck**
✓ **Playing with hair**
✓ **Blinking more than usual**
✓ **Wringing hands**
✓ **Not looking directly at you**

OTHER SIGNS TO LOOK OUT FOR:

Note their tone of voice. Do they look happy when they're talking about something sad? Are they nodding but saying no?

Are they too still? If a liar is smart, he or she might try and stay still to avoid looking shifty. If you notice that people aren't moving, or that they're talking in one tone of voice, they could be up to no good!

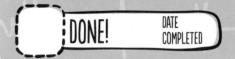

DONE!   DATE COMPLETED

MEASURE RAINFALL 89

You don't need a lot of expensive equipment to learn about the weather. Try making a simple rain gauge, and start keeping track of rainfall in your area.

1 Cut the top off an empty 2-liter bottle and weigh the bottle down with some stones. Flip the top section upside down and pop it back inside to make a funnel.

2 Mark a scale in inches, or divisions of inches, on the side of your gauge, using a waterproof marker and a ruler.

3 Write down the amount of rainfall you see on a graph, or a simple chart. Mark the days of the week along the bottom axis, and write the amount of rainfall along the side axis.

WHY NOT?
Ask friends or relatives to keep track of rainfall where they live and compare notes!

DONE! DATE COMPLETED

90 DESIGN A COAT OF ARMS

A traditional coat of arms is a decorated shield that features all kinds of things related to your family. Try making your very own!

1 First draw a basic shape for your coat of arms. The most common shapes are shown above, or you can design your own!

2 Write a list of words that spring to mind when you think about your family. These will make up the symbols of your shield! Write down the name of each family member and something cool about them.

3 Split your coat of arms into sections, one for each member of your family. Now take one thing about them from your list and draw it into that section.

WHY NOT?
Add a family motto to your coat of arms, such as "Friday night is movie night!"

DONE!   DATE COMPLETED

SPIN A BASKETBALL ON YOUR FINGERTIP

91

Practice makes perfect with this tricky skill, but soon you'll impress everyone with your spinning style!

1 Holding the basketball in one hand, take the opposite hand and spin the ball fast. Use any of the fingers on that hand to hold up the ball as it spins, but your index finger might be the easiest.

2 Gently pat the ball on the side as you spin it on the pad of your index finger. Wait for one second, and then spin again.

3 Keep your elbows bent and tuck your chin under so that you remain steady. Try to spin longer each time!

TIP!
Deflate the ball slightly before you begin. This will create a larger surface area when you touch it, and will help you control it better!

 DONE!   DATE COMPLETED

92 MAKE A RECYCLED BIRD FEEDER

Looking for birds in your backyard? Encourage winged visitors to stop by for a rest or a snack!

YOU WILL NEED:

- Empty, clean juice carton
- Paint and paintbrush
- Scissors
- Glue
- Hole punch
- Popsicle stick
- Birdseed
- Heavy-duty string

1 Paint and decorate the outside of the carton and let it dry.

2 Carefully cut a rectangle in the bottom of the carton for your birds to hop in and out of!

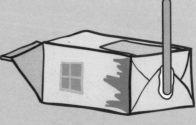

3 Glue your Popsicle stick to the bottom of your carton. This will make a perch for your birds to land on!

4 Punch a hole in the top of your carton, and feed some sturdy string through the hole.

5 Fill the bottom of the carton with birdseed and hang it from the branch of a tree. Watch as the hungry birds come to visit!

WHY NOT?
Keep a diary of all the different types of birds that visit your feeder!

DONE!

DATE COMPLETED

93 BUILD AN EXTREME INDOOR DEN

What's better on a rainy day than a super-sized homemade den? Gather some blankets, cushions, and chairs to see what you can make!

Put all breakable objects away. Try not to use weak or small pieces of furniture that might fall down on the people inside the den.

Drape blankets, sheets, and towels over large pieces of furniture like a dining table, the back of an armchair, or sofa.

Use chairs to prop up your sheets. Turn them around so they can be used as tables inside the den.

Sheets make the best roofs because they are light. Keep them in place with clips or cushions.

Fill your den with fun things to do. Books, games, and snacks are perfect!

The inside of your den must be comfy and cozy. Fill the floor with cushions so that you've always got somewhere comfy to sit.

DONE!   DATE COMPLETED

ENTERTAIN YOURSELF

If you're alone, there's no reason to be bored! Even when you're all by yourself, there is always something fun to do.

1 Bounce and hit a tennis ball against a wall. How many times can you hit it in a row?

2 Twirl a Hula-Hoop indoors or out. How long can you keep it spinning without dropping it?

3 Make up a dance routine to your favorite song.

4 Find three things in your bedroom that could be used to make instruments.

5 Create a small shadow puppet theater using a box, a flashlight, and some small toy figures.

6 Find a book you've never read before and start it.

7 Write a letter to yourself in the future.

8 Invent and draw your own comic book character.

DONE!

DATE COMPLETED

95 MAKE HOMEMADE LEMONADE

What could be better than a glass of cool, homemade lemonade on a hot summer day? This recipe makes enough for six glasses.

YOU WILL NEED:

- 8 lemons
- 6 cups of water
- 1¼ cups of sugar

1 Squeeze the juice of your lemons into a large pitcher—make sure you take out any seeds!

2 Ask an adult to heat a third of the water in a pan with the sugar. Keep stirring until the sugar has completely dissolved, then mix with the lemon juice.

3 Add the rest of the water to the pitcher, then leave in the refrigerator to chill. Serve with ice and a slice of lemon.

DONE!   DATE COMPLETED

PLAY WITH PHYSICS

96

Try this cool trick to see how the energy from one falling ball can be transferred to another.

1 For this experiment you will need a basketball (or something similar, like a soccer ball) and a tennis ball.

2 Hold the tennis ball over the basketball and drop both at the same time.

3 The basketball should stop, but the tennis ball should launch itself upward as the energy from the basketball transfers to it.

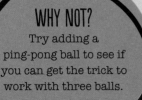

WHY NOT?
Try adding a ping-pong ball to see if you can get the trick to work with three balls.

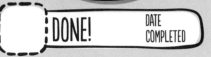

DONE!   DATE COMPLETED

97 MASTER THE ART OF ORIGAMI

Origami is the ancient Japanese art of paper folding. You'll be amazed at what you can make from just a simple square of paper. Why not start by making this cute rabbit?

1 Take a square of paper and fold it in half diagonally.

2 Open the paper out, then fold the corners inward toward the center fold.

3 Fold down the top corner to make a triangle.

4 Fold the tip of the top flap back to make the tail.

5 Fold in half along the center fold.

6 Your paper should now look like this.

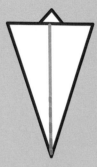

7 Use scissors to make a small cut a third of the way along the center fold. This will make the rabbit's ears.

8 Next bend back each of the ears.

9 Fold the bottom corners under. This will make your rabbit sit up.

10 Fold the ears down. You now have your very own origami rabbit!

WHY NOT?
Try using different-colored paper and draw some details on your new creation!

DONE!

DATE COMPLETED

98 PLAY WATER-BALLOON VOLLEYBALL

This is the perfect game to play on a hot day at the beach, in the park, or even in your backyard. But watch out—you're going to get wet!

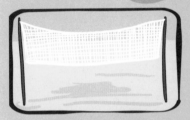

1 Set up your net and gather your players. You'll need at least four people to play this game.

2 Get a pile of water balloons ready.

3 Each team grabs a beach towel or blanket and uses it to launch a balloon over the net for the other team, which has to try and catch it in its towel. The winning team is the one that bursts the fewest balloons (and stays the driest!).

WHY NOT?
Double the fun and try playing with two water balloons at the same time!

 DONE!   DATE COMPLETED

MAKE YOUR OWN BOOMERANG

Boomerangs are throwing sticks traditionally used by Australian aborigines. Make this cool three-winged version from a simple piece of cardboard.

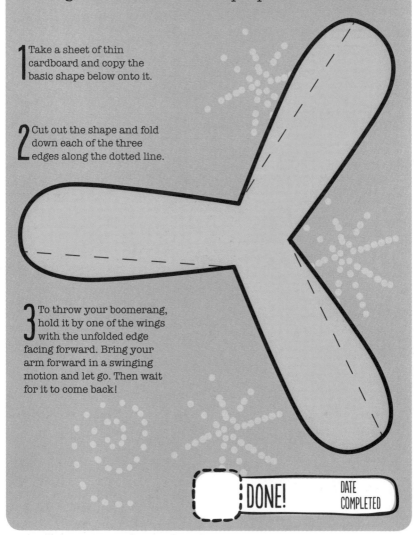

1 Take a sheet of thin cardboard and copy the basic shape below onto it.

2 Cut out the shape and fold down each of the three edges along the dotted line.

3 To throw your boomerang, hold it by one of the wings with the unfolded edge facing forward. Bring your arm forward in a swinging motion and let go. Then wait for it to come back!

DONE!

DATE COMPLETED

100 FIND YOUR CHINESE ZODIAC ANIMAL

The Chinese zodiac is ancient, but it is just as meaningful today! Look up the year you were born—which animal are you?

RAT

2008, 1996, 1984, 1972

Your intelligence makes you a great speaker, and you have a very busy social life.

OX

2009, 1997, 1985, 1973

You are strong, steady, and reliable. But most importantly, you have a lot of patience.

TIGER

2010, 1998, 1986, 1974

Ambition and confidence make you a great leader. You are also brave and generous!

RABBIT

2011, 1999, 1987, 1975

You are strong-willed, elegant, and kind—and you hate disagreements!

DRAGON

2012, 2000, 1988, 1976

You have an A+ imagination and like to meet all of your goals.

SNAKE

2013, 2001, 1989, 1977

You are a super-organized communicator who likes to think serious thoughts.

HORSE

2002, 1990, 1978, 1966

You work very hard but are always up for a wild, warm-hearted adventure.

RAM

2015, 2003, 1991, 1979

You stay calm—even in a crisis. You are always generous, too!

MONKEY

2016, 2004, 1992, 1980,

You have a bright wit and know how to turn on the charm. You're always on the move!

ROOSTER

2017, 2005, 1993, 1981

You are very dignified, and usually love to be the focus of attention! You are also generous and well-meaning.

DOG

2018, 2006, 1994, 1982

You seem to have a lot of luck! You're also honest and wise beyond your years.

PIG

2019, 2007, 1995, 1983

Your determination and spirit helps others. You always know how to stay positive.

DONE!

DATE COMPLETED

101 MAKE A PAPIER-MÂCHÉ BOWL

Follow these simple steps to transform old newspapers into these colorful bowls. Why not make one as a gift for a friend?

YOU WILL NEED:

- A bowl to use as a mold
- Plastic wrap
- Newspapers cut into strips
- Craft glue mixed with water
- Scissors
- Paint and a paintbrush
- Clear varnish

1 Cover a bowl with plastic wrap. The plastic wrap will stop the papier-mâché from sticking to the bowl once it has dried.

2 Start by brushing the newspaper strips with the watered-down craft glue and overlapping them on the outside of the bowl.

3 Once you've covered the bowl in newspaper, leave it to dry for a couple of hours before adding another layer. Make sure the strips aren't too wet or they won't dry flat.

4 After you've built up a few layers of paper, allow them to dry out completely before removing the papier-mâché from the mold. Trim the edges with scissors.

5 Now it's time to decorate your creation! You can use paint, glitter, or even add a few more layers of colored paper for a cool collage effect.

WHY NOT?
Try making a matching set of bowls in different sizes.

6 Finish your bowls with a coat of clear varnish. If you don't have varnish, then a coat of normal craft glue will also give a shiny finish.

DONE! | DATE COMPLETED

STAYING SAFE: DOS AND DON'TS

DO: Be careful when using scissors, and other sharp objects.

DO: Wear a helmet while riding a bike or a skateboard.

DO: Always wear old clothes or an apron when doing art projects.

DO: Carefully follow the instructions and pay attention to any safety warnings.

DON'T: Start a messy project without asking an adult.

DON'T: Go anywhere without telling an adult first!

ACKNOWLEDGMENTS

Written by Laura Dower
Editors: Alexandra Koken, Gemma Barder, and Fay Evans
Design and Illustration: Dan Bramall and Katie Knutton

Elements of illustration for activities 38, 41, 55, and 61, 64, 96, and 100 from Shutterstock.